は　し　が　き

　本書は、世界のニュースを通して Reading, Listening, Speaking, Writing のバランスのとれた学習が効果的にできるように工夫してあります。2019年５月：上流階級育ちの坊ちゃんの中身のない自信に気をつけろ、10月：ラグビー「桜戦士」、チームの結束を称賛；日本のファンは歴史的成果を褒めちぎる；iPhoneのはるか前に無線社会の基礎を築いた人たち；「飛び恥」が航空業界に打撃、11月：日本の報道機関、自国の将来に確信が無い；コアラが森林火災の犠牲に；英語教育改革を凍結させてはいけない、12月：ノート型パソコンのリサイクルでの代償：タイで有毒ガスが；生徒の読解力を測る国際的試験で日本は過去最低の水準に落ちた；移民流入は壁では阻止できない；新国籍法への反対運動が荒れ狂うが、インドはヒンドゥ教国となるのか、2020年１月：サウジ社会の変化はコーヒーハウスを覗けば分かる；カルロス・ゴーンの大脱走劇、２月：ソマリアの若者たち、政府機能不全の地域に足を踏み入れる、３月：疫病の渦中で必要なのはフランスではペストリーとワイン、米国ではゴルフと銃、４月：他の人たちよりもずっと感染力が強い人たちがいる理由；急激な変化：ガイアナは石油で裕福になったが、民族間の緊張も増大、まで世界中のニュースを満載しております。

　The New York Times, The New York Times International Edition, The Japan Times, The Guardian, The Times, The Express & Star から社会・文化・政治経済・情報・言語・教育・科学・医学・環境・娯楽・スポーツなどのあらゆる分野を網羅しましたので、身近に世界中のニュースに触れ、読み、聞き、話し、書く楽しさを育みながら、多角的にそして複眼的に英語運用力が自然に培われるように意図しています。

　15課より構成され、各課に新聞記事読解前にBefore you readを設けました。本文の内容が予想できる写真と、どこにあるかを示す地図と国の情報を参照しながら自由に意見交換をします。次の Words and Phrases では、記事に記載されている単語や熟語とそれに合致する英語の説明を選び、あらかじめ大事な語の理解を深めて行きます。Summaryでは記事の内容を予想しながら、５語を適当な箇所に記入して要約文を完成させます。記事読解前では難しいようであれば、読解後に活用しても良いと思います。さらに、記事に関連した裏話も載せました。記事の読解にあたり、わかり易い註釈を記事の右端に付け、理解度をチェックするための Multiple Choice, True or False, 記事に関連した語法を学ぶVocabularyと豊富に取り揃えました。Summaryと記事がそのまま音声化されたファイルをウェブ上にあげています。多方面に渡る記事やExercisesを活用して、英字新聞に慣れ親しみ、使っていただけることを望んでいます。

　今回テキスト作成に際して、お世話になりました朝日出版社社長原雅久氏、編集部の日比野忠氏、小川洋一郎氏に心からお礼申し上げます。

2020年10月

高橋　優身
伊藤　典子
Richard Powell

CONTENTS

15 Selected Units of English through the News Media

—2021 Edition—

Masami Takahashi

Noriko Itoh

Richard Powell

Asahi Press

記事提供
The New York Times
The Times
The Japan Times
The Guardian
Bloomberg
The Express & Star
Kyodo
AFP-JIJI

写真提供
アフロ：The New York Times／Redux／
ロイター／Splash／AP／TT News Agency／
Kyodo News

地図・イラスト
ヨシオカユリ

15 Selected Units of English through the News Media -2021 Edition-

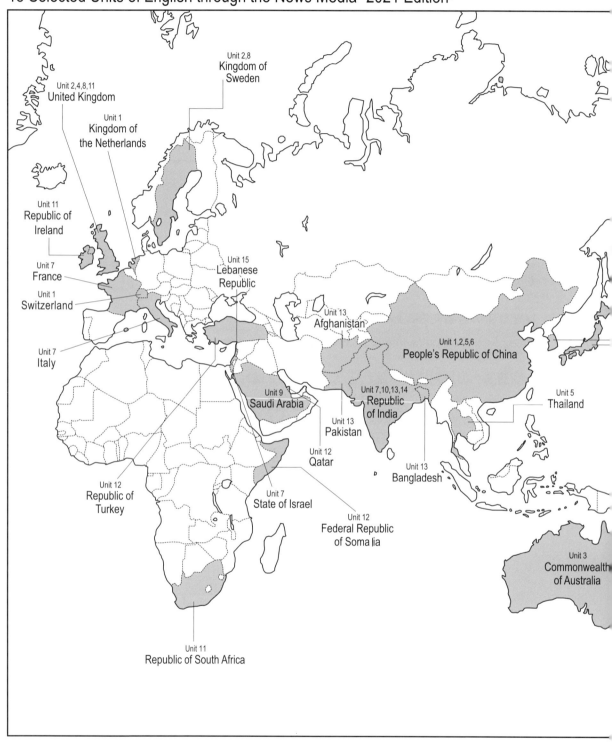

Unit 2,8
Kingdom of
Sweden

Unit 2,4,8,11
United Kingdom

Unit 1
Kingdom of
the Netherlands

Unit 11
Republic of
Ireland

Unit 7
France

Unit 1
Switzerland

Unit 15
Lebanese
Republic

Unit 13
Afghanistan

Unit 1,2,5,6
People's Republic of China

Unit 7
Italy

Unit 9
Saudi Arabia

Unit 7,10,13,14
Republic
of India

Unit 5
Thailand

Unit 13
Pakistan

Unit 12
Qatar

Unit 13
Bangladesh

Unit 12
Republic of
Turkey

Unit 7
State of Israel

Unit 12
Federal Republic
of Soma lia

Unit 3
Commonwealth
of Australia

Unit 11
Republic of South Africa

Unit 1,6,10
South Korea

Unit 1,2,8,11,15
Japan

Unit 2,6,7,8,10,13,15
U.S.A.

Unit 10
United Mexican
States

Unit 14
Republic of Guyana

Unit 11
New Zealand

音声再生アプリ「リスニング・トレーナー」を使った 音声ダウンロード

朝日出版社開発のアプリ、「リスニング・トレーナー（リストレ）」を使えば、教科書の音声をスマホ、タブレットに簡単にダウンロードできます。どうぞご活用ください。

◉ アプリ【リスニング・トレーナー】の使い方

《アプリのダウンロード》

App Store または Google Play から「リスニング・トレーナー」のアプリ（無料）をダウンロード

App Storeは
こちら▶

Google Playは
こちら▶

《アプリの使い方》

① アプリを開き「コンテンツを追加」をタップ
② 画面上部に【15664】を入力しDoneをタップ

音声ストリーミング配信 》》》

この教科書の音声は、右記ウェブサイトにて無料で配信しています。

https://text.asahipress.com/free/english/

15 Selected Units of
English through the News Media

- 英語教育改革を凍結させてはいけない
- 生徒の読解力を測る国際的試験で日本は過去最低水準に落ちた

平均得点の国際比較

順位	科学的応用力		読解力		数学的応用力	
1	(10)北京・上海・江蘇・浙江※	590	(27)北京・上海・江蘇・浙江※	555	(6)北京・上海・江蘇・浙江※	591
2	(1)シンガポール	551	(1)シンガポール	549	(1)シンガポール	569
3	(6)マ カ オ	544	(12)マ カ オ	525	(3)マ カ オ	558
4	(3)エストニア	530	(2)香 港	524	(2)香 港	551
5	(2)日 本	529	(6)エストニア	523	(4)台 湾	531
6	(5)フィンランド	522	(3)カ ナ ダ	520	(5)日 本	527
7	(11)韓 国	519	(4)フィンランド	520	(7)韓 国	526
8	(7)カ ナ ダ	518	(5)アイルランド	518	(9)エストニア	523
9	(9)香 港	517	(7)韓 国	514	(11)オランダ	519
10	(4)台 湾	516	(13)ポーランド	512	(17)ポーランド	516
	OECD平均	489	**15**(8)日 本	504	OECD平均	489
			OECD平均	487		

(　)は前回順位、小数点以下は四捨五入、※前回は北京・上海・江蘇・広東として参加

日本の読解力15位、上位層と差を示す PISA の平均得点の国際比較

Photo: Kyodo News

Before you read

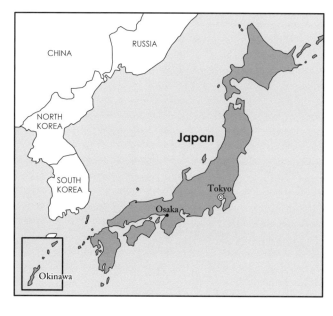

Japan　日本国

面積　377,961.73km²（世界61位）
人口　126,860,000人（世界11位）
　　　日本民族　98.5%
　　　朝鮮人　0.5%
　　　中国人　0.4%
首都　東京都
最大都市　大阪市（昼間人口）
　　　　　横浜市（夜間人口）
　　　　　東京都23区部
GDP　4兆9,718億ドル（世界3位）
　　　1人当たりの GDP　39,304ドル
　　　　　　　　　　　　（世界26位）
通貨　円
公用語　なし、事実上日本語
宗教　無宗教信者　52%
　　　仏教　35%　/ 神道　4%
　　　キリスト教　2.3%
政治　立憲君主制
識字率　99.8%

Words and Phrases

次の１～５の語の説明として最も近いものをa～eから１つ選び、（　）内に記入しなさい。

1. assess	（　　）		**a.**	achievement or skill
2. discriminate	（　　）		**b.**	join or be involved
3. proficiency	（　　）		**c.**	trustworthiness
4. credibility	（　　）		**d.**	evaluate or measure
5. participate	（　　）		**e.**	treat unfairly

Summary

次の英文は記事の要約です。下の語群から最も適切な語を１つ選び、（　）内に記入しなさい。

02

Although still above the OECD (　　　　　), Japan dropped seven places in international (　　　　　) for reading skills. Students appear to be especially poor at reading long (　　　　　) on computers. There was even worse news for English skills, with one body (　　　　) Japan 53 out of 100. Meanwhile the Ministry of Education is (　　　　) to reform university entrance exams.

average	placing	rankings	struggling	texts

2020年度からスタートする大学入学共通テストで、英語民間試験の活用が見送られることになった。試験に向けて努力を積み重ねてきた高校生の間には、困惑が広がっている。

大学入試センター試験に代わる大学入学共通テストは、小中高校教育の転換も目指していて、中心が数学や国語への記述式問題採用と英語の「読む・聞く・話す・書く」の４技能を測る民間試験の活用だった。英検、TOEFL iBT, GTEC, TEAP, TEAP CBT, IELTS, Cambridge の７種類の英語民間試験から、受験生本人が選び、４月から12月の間に２回まで受けることができる。この英語民間試験を活用するには、実施会場が都市部に偏り、地方在住の受験生には負担が大きい、また受験料が高額で２回で約５万円もかかる、試験の難易度が異なり複数試験の比較が難しい、試験ごとに異なる採点基準、不正や機器トラブルなどへの対応など課題が山積みである。文科省は、英語入学試験を2024年度開始と掲げているが、生徒が身に着けた英語力をきちんと評価できる試験を検討してもらいたい。

OECD が79か国・地域の15歳計約60万人を対象に2018年に実施した PISA 国際学習到達度調査の結果を公表したが、日本は「読解力」が15位で2015年の８位から大きく順位を下げた。正答率が低かったのは、文章から必要な情報を探り出したり、文章の信用性を吟味したりする問題だった。スマートフォンの普及により、仲間同士の短文や絵文字のやりとりが中心になり、長い文章をきちんと読む機会が減っているのも原因の１つだ。

Reading

03

Don't freeze English education reform

The government last week announced it was putting off the planned introduction of private-sector English proficiency tests as part of standardized university entrance exams next April after the new system was criticized for many problems
5 regarding access to testing locations and higher examination fees.

The current English-language component of the standardized entrance exams only assesses reading and listening comprehension. By using private-sector tests that also check
10 writing and speaking ability, there were great expectations that students would be evaluated in a more comprehensive manner and thereby would prepare better to communicate in English.

04

Under the proposed system, six private-sector institutions
15 were to provide seven kinds of tests, including the GTEC (Global Test of English Communication), TOEFL, Cambridge English test and Japan's Eiken test starting next April.

But some critics said the new system would discriminate against students in remote areas because not all of the
20 proficiency tests would be offered in every prefecture. The fees for taking the exams also varied, with some costing over ¥20,000. This meant students from wealthy families and those living in big cities will have had an advantage.

In recent years, China, South Korea and many other non-
05 25 English speaking countries have been pushing hard to enhance their English education, and as a result their skills appear to have improved dramatically.

English proficiency rankings illustrate this trend. A 2019 study by EF Education First, a Switzerland-based company
30 that offers language training, ranked the Netherlands at the top of 100 countries surveyed. Looking at Asian countries, Japan came in at a lowly 53rd, far behind South Korea at 37th

putting off 〜：〜を延期する

introduction：導入

private-sector：民間の

proficiency tests：検定試験

standardized：共通の

component：構成要素

comprehensive：総合的な

GTEC：ジーテック《ベネッセコーポレーションが実施している英語4技能検定》

TOEFL：トフル《第2言語としての英語のテスト；米国大学や大学院に入学希望する外国人用》

Cambridge English test：ケンブリッジ英検《ケンブリッジ大学英語検定機構が実施》

Eiken test：英検《日本英語検定協会が実施》

discriminate against 〜：〜に不公平な取り扱いをする

pushing hard：大いに推進する

enhance 〜：〜を強化する

EF Education First：イーエフ《1965年、スウェーデンで創立の私立語学学校》

and China at 40th.

The Japan Times, November 8, 2019

In international test, Japan sinks to lowest-ever rank for students' reading skills

In a triennial international survey on academic ability, Japanese students ranked at their lowest level ever for reading skills while remaining in the top band for science and mathematics, the OECD said Tuesday.

The 2018 Program for International Student Assessment tests covered about 600,000 15-year-old students in 79 countries and regions.

Japanese students came 15th in reading — down from eighth in the 2015 tests.

They scored 504 points on average for reading skills, which was higher than the average score of 487 among the 37 OECD members, but down by 12 points from the previous test.

The education ministry believes students can still improve in their ability to find information from texts, as well as better evaluate the credibility of texts and more clearly explain their thoughts and reasoning to others. It also pointed out that Japanese students are not used to reading long passages on computer screens.

Students in Japan also ranked lower for science — in fifth place, down from second — and mathematics — at sixth, down from fifth.

Beijing, Shanghai, Jiangsu province and Zhejiang province, which jointly participated in the tests as one region, finished first in the three fields. Singapore, which came first in the 2015 tests, ranked second in the three categories.

The Japan Times based on JIJI, December 4, 2019

triennial：3年に一度の

academic ability：学力

science：理科

OECD：経済協力開発機構

Program for International Student Assessment：生徒の学習到達度調査 (PISA)

education ministry：文部科学省

credibility：信頼性

reasoning：推論

are not used to ～ ing：～することに慣れていない

Beijing：北京

Jiangsu province：江蘇省

Zhejiang province：浙江省

fields：分野

categories：部門《fields と同じ》

Exercises

次の１〜４の英文を完成させ、５の英文の質問に答えるために、 a〜d の中から最も適切なものを１つ選びなさい。

1. The article about 'English education reform' states that

    a. private sector English proficiency tests are creative and will work well for students.

    b. the high fees are a guarantee for acquiring greater students.

    c. these tests are located in very convenient facilities.

    d. there were plans for more comprehensive testing.

2. The top country for English proficiency according to the 2019 study was

    a. the Netherlands.

    b. Switzerland.

    c. South Korea.

    d. China.

3. The International Student Assessment was given to:

    a. 20,000 students.

    b. 60,000 students.

    c. 200,000 students.

    d. 600,000 students.

4. A problem that the lowered test scores may reflect was

    a. students' discomfort at reading long passages on computer screens.

    b. poor directions by the administrator.

    c. crowded testing sites in distant areas.

    d. expensive exam fees.

5. How many different English-language skills were to be tested in students?

    a. Two.

    b. Four.

    c. Five.

    d. Seven.

本文の内容に合致するものに T（True）、合致しないものに F（False）をつけなさい。

(   ) **1.** Japanese students had disappointing scores on the International Students Assessment tests.

(   ) **2.** The country that finished first in reading, mathematics, and science is Singapore.

(   ) **3.** South Korea has been pushing to enhance their English education.

(   ) **4.** The government planned to take out English reading and listening tests and replace them with speaking and writing ability tests.

(   ) **5.** The new plan for testing will continue as scheduled next April.

Vocabulary

次の 1 ～ 8 は、「read」に関する英文です。日本文に合わせて（   ）内に最も適切な語を下の語群から 1 つ選び、記入しなさい。

1. 母は、私たちによく読み聞かせをしてくれた。
Our mother used to read (   ) us.

2. 友人が肝臓ガンで亡くなったことを新聞で知った。
I read (   ) the paper that my friend died of a liver cancer.

3. 手相を見ましょうか？
Can I (   ) your palm?

4. 彼女の答えは、辞退だと思った。
I read her reply (   ) a refusal.

5. 行間を読む必要がある。
You have to read (   ) the lines.

6. 娘は、4 歳なのに文字がよく読める。
My daughter reads (   ) for a four-year-old.

7. その議事録を読まれたものとみなして良いだろう。
We can (   ) the minutes as read.

8. 朝 1 時間読書するのを習慣にしている。
I (   ) a rule of reading an hour in the morning.

as	between	in	make
read	take	to	well

- 日本の報道機関、自国の将来に確信が無い
- 「飛び恥」が航空業界に打撃

米国の学校での気候変動を巡る集会にグレタさんも参加し、発言する

Photo: ロイター／アフロ

Before you read

1. What do you think the article will be about?

    この記事は何の話題についてだと思いますか？

2. What do you know about Greta Thunberg?

    グレタ・トゥーンベリについて何か知っていますか？

次の１〜５の語の説明として最も近いものをａ〜ｅから１つ選び、（　　）内に記入しなさい。

1. launch　　　（　　）　　　**a.** initiate
2. appall　　　（　　）　　　**b.** except in the case of
3. barring　　　（　　）　　　**c.** lonely
4. forlorn　　　（　　）　　　**d.** sharp rise
5. spike　　　（　　）　　　**e.** shock

Summary

次の英文は記事の要約です。下の語群から最も適切な語を１つ選び、（　　）内に記入しなさい。

08

　A recent report involving 153 countries (　　　　　) that little has been done to tackle climate change, (　　　　) 40 years of discussion. Greta Thunberg, and thousands who follow the young Swedish activist, (　　　　). (　　　　　) airlines are recognizing the need to reduce carbon emissions. But the US president is withdrawing his country from international (　　　　) programs.

agree　　concludes　　despite　　environmental　　even

　2003年１月３日、スウェーデンの首都ストックホルムで、環境活動家の Greta Ernman Thunberg グレタ・エルンマン・トゥーンベリが誕生した。彼女の母親は、著名なオペラ歌手、父親は俳優である。
　彼女が８歳のときに、気候変動について知り、落ち込んで無気力になった。その後、アスペルガー症候群、強迫性障害、選択的無言症と診断された。診断から２年後、菜食主義者となり、飛行機には乗らず、彼女の言動に家族の同意を求めた。アスペルガーを病気とみなさず、代わりに「スーパーパワー」と呼び始めた。
　そして、グレタが15歳の時に、気候変動に対するストライキとスピーチを学校で開始した。スウェーデン議会前に一人で座り込み、より強い気候変動対策を求める活動を始めた。「Friday for future 未来のための金曜日」という名で、気候変動学校スト運動を組織した。その後、国連の「気候変動サミット」でグレタが演説した後、世界160か国以上で温暖化対策の強化を求める抗議デモが行われた。グレタは、SNS などで世界の注目を集め、「グレタ・トゥーンベリ効果」と呼ばれ、多くの学生や政治家たちに大きな影響を与えている。COP24などの国際会議に招かれ、演説を行った。温室効果ガスを大量に排出するとして飛行機の利用を避け、サミット出席のために英国からヨットで２週間かけて大西洋を横断した。

Reading

09

News outlets are uncertain about the nation's future

"How dare you?" demanded Greta Thunberg of world leaders at the U.N. in September. The 16-year-old Swedish climate activist was furious. "All you can talk about," she said, "is money and fairy tales about eternal economic growth."

⁵ That's all there *is* to talk about, U.S. President Donald Trump in effect replied to her last week, formally launching his country's withdrawal from the green-house-gas-limiting Paris agreement.

The next day, as though in reply to *him*, a global team
¹⁰ of 11,258 scientists in 153 countries declared a climate emergency of appalling proportions, foreseeing "untold human suffering," barring vast changes not at present on the horizon. "Despite 40 years of global climate negotiations, with few exceptions, we have generally conducted business
¹⁵ as usual and have largely failed to address this predicament," the report said.

Thunberg's activism began in August 2018 with lonely sit-ins in front of the Swedish parliament. Her placard read, "Schools strike for climate." She cut a forlorn figure. Did
²⁰ she foresee then the global movement she now leads? "The movement's momentum has even reached Japan," Metropolis magazine observed acidly this past August. Fridays for Future Tokyo held its first rally in February—"its 20 or so student protesters outnumbered by reporters." Organizers persisted
²⁵ and the numbers rose—to thousands at best, compared to tens of thousands elsewhere in the world.

"I wanted to change people's awareness like Greta, but I couldn't," organizer Sayaka Miyazaki, a 22-year-old Rikkyo University student, lamented to the Asahi Shimbun in
³⁰ September.

She may yet. Greta didn't become Greta overnight.

The Japan Times, November 17, 2019

News outlets：報道機関

That's all there *is* to talk about：国連では相変わらずに今もお金と経済成長しか話題にならない

green-house-gas：温室効果ガス《温室効果の原因となる気体；一酸化炭素、二酸化炭素、フロン、メタンなど》

Paris agreement：パリ協定

appalling proportions：最悪の比率であること

on the horizon：近い将来の

address 〜：〜に取り組む、対処する

activism：積極的行動

lonely sit-ins：一人での座り込み抗議

cut a forlorn figure：孤独で寂しそうに見えた

Metropolis：メトロポリス《東京に在住する英語を話す外国人を対象とする無料の月刊雑誌》

Fridays for Future Tokyo：「未来のための金曜日東京・グローバル気候マーチ」日本で主催する団体

student protesters：学生から成るデモ参加者

awareness：意識

yet：いつか

'Flight-shaming' could slow growth of airline industry, says IATA

| Climate now 'top of the agenda' for investors as airlines try to lower carbon emissions

Flight-shaming：飛び恥

IATA：国際航空運送協会

top of the agenda：第一検討事項

carbon emissions：炭素排出量

Escalating pressure from investors is pushing airlines to address environmental concerns, according to the International Air Transport Association (IATA), which acknowledged that the trend toward "flight-shaming" could weigh on the industry's future growth.

Speaking at a conference in London where airlines vied to demonstrate plans to decarbonise, IATA said the climate was now "top of the agenda" for investors.

Citing HSBC research, IATA's chief economist, Brian Pearce, said climate issues came up an average of seven times on each call between European airlines and investors in 2019, compared with an average of less than once per earnings call between 2013 and 2017.

Pearce said: "Climate change is not just an issue for protestors or scientists. You can see the spike this year. This is on the top of the agenda for mainstream investors now. We're getting pressure from all quarters."

He said *flygskam*, or flight-shaming—the trend towards making air travel socially unacceptable due to its carbon cost — "could be a factor slowing growth in the future."

Although airlines have signed up to Corsia offsetting scheme set up by the UN aviation agency, ICAO, many believe taxes and a consumer backlash could grow. Shai Weiss, Virgin Atlantic's chief executive, said: "If there is one name everyone in the airline industry knows today that it perhaps didn't know a year ago, it's Greta Thunberg."

The Guardian, October 17, 2019

environmental concerns：環境問題

weigh on ～：～を圧迫する

vied to ～：争って～した

decarbonise：化石燃料依存から脱却する、脱炭素化する

HSBC：香港上海銀行《ロンドンに本社を置く世界的な金融持株会社》

came up on ～：～に出た

call：コールオプション《指定期間内の指定価格での「買い付け」》

earnings call：（投資家向けの）収支報告、業績発表

due to its carbon cost：炭素排出という代償のせいで

Corsia：国際航空のための炭素相殺計画

ICAO：国際民間航空機関

consumer backlash：消費者からの反発

Virgin Atlantic：ヴァージン・アトランティック航空《大陸間の長距離国際線をメインに運航する英国の航空会社》

Exercises

次の１〜５の英文を完成させるために、ａ〜ｄの中から最も適切なものを１つ選びなさい。

1. Greta Thunberg feels that

   a. the world must seriously deal with climate change.

   b. the world is seriously dealing with the problem of climate change.

   c. governments need to focus more on economic growth.

   d. President Trump has not focused enough on economic growth.

2. Sayaka Miyazaki has expressed her feelings of

   a. happiness about the success of ecological movements.

   b. boredom with talking to citizens about the future.

   c. disappointment at being unable to persuade more people.

   d. sadness over Greta Thunberg's recent inactivity.

3. One thing that airlines fear may reduce their profits in future is

   a. the rising price of fuel.

   b. the environmental cost of carbon.

   c. lower taxes on passengers.

   d. lower support for Thunberg.

4. Investors are becoming more interested in

   a. financial profits and losses.

   b. environmental repercussions from flying.

   c. the financial benefits of higher taxes.

   d. the dangers of decarbonizing flights.

5. The word "flygskam" refers to

   a. airline travel becoming socially unacceptable.

   b. the low effect of carbon on our environment.

   c. consumers' rising demand for flights.

   d. all of the above statements.

本文の内容に合致するものに T (True)、合致しないものに F (False) をつけなさい。

(   ) **1.** People will probably be flying more often with reduced airline ticket prices.

(   ) **2.** Greta Thunberg spoke to the U.N. and reprimanded them for not focusing on climate change.

(   ) **3.** A report says that environmental changes have been ignored for more than 60 years.

(   ) **4.** Greta Thunberg made a huge impact on the world, including investors.

(   ) **5.** When Greta first started fighting to make people aware of climate change, she was not a popular speaker.

Vocabulary

次の英文は、the Japan Times に掲載された *Greta Thunberg and German railway engage in raging 'tweetstorm'* 『グレタ・トゥーンベリとドイツ鉄道会社が荒れ狂ったツイートストームに取り組む』の記事の一部です。下の語群から最も適切なものを１つ選び、（   ）内に記入しなさい。

Climate activist Greta Thunberg and Germany's national railway company created a tweetstorm Sunday after she (   ) a photo of herself sitting on the (   ) of a train surrounded by lots of bags. The image has drawn plenty of comment online about the performance of German railways. Thunberg posted the tweet late Saturday with the comment "traveling on overcrowded (   ) through Germany. And I'm finally on my way home!"

But German railway company suggested that Thunberg may not have spent the whole time sitting on the floor. And the 16-year-old Swedish activist later sought to draw a line under the matter by tweeting that she eventually got a (   ) and that overcrowded trains are a good thing. Some Twitter users expressed (   ) for Thunberg for not being able to get a proper seat on the train for the long ride home from Madrid, where she was attending months of traveling by trains and (   ) to different climate events in Europe and the United States.

Thunberg doesn't fly on planes because it's considered (   ) to the climate. Last week, she was named Time magazine's Person of the Year for her efforts to (   ) government and others to take faster actions in fighting climate change.

boats	floor	harmful	pity
posted	prod	seat	trains

●コアラが森林火災の犠牲に

オーストラリア東部の山火事でコアラ病院に保護され、手当てを受ける絶滅危惧種のコアラ

Photo: Splash ／アフロ

Before you read

Commonwealth of Australia
オーストラリア 連邦
英連邦王国の一国

面積 7,692,024km²（日本の約20倍）（世界６位）
人口 24,990,000人（世界55位）
民族 ヨーロッパ系 80%
　　　アジア系 12% ／ アボリジニ 2%
首都 キャンベラ
最大都市 シドニー
公用語 英語
宗教 キリスト教 52%
　　　（カトリック 25.8% ／ 聖公会 18.7%）
　　　非キリスト教 5% ／ 無宗教 30%
識字率 99%
政体 立憲君主制
GDP 1兆3,379億米ドル（世界14位）
　　　1人当たり GDP 55,707米ドル（世界11位）
通貨 オーストラリア・ドル

Words and Phrases

次の１～５の語の説明として最も近いものをａ～ｅから１つ選び、（　）内に記入しなさい。

1. plight　　　　（　　）　　　**a.** thoroughly burn

2. singe　　　　（　　）　　　**b.** wrap in cloth

3. swaddle　　　（　　）　　　**c.** bad situation

4. incinerate　（　　）　　　**d.** psychological pain

5. distress　　　（　　）　　　**e.** partly burn

Summary

　次の英文は記事の要約です。下の語群から最も適切な語を１つ選び、（　）内に記入しなさい。

14

　Koalas are among the worst (　　　　　　) of terrible fires that have destroyed millions of (　　　　　　) of Australian forest. Fires are (　　　　　　) in Australia, and although koalas do not run away like kangaroos or snakes, they do have some defense (　　　　　　). But the intensity of recent conflagrations has been too much for a (　　　　　　) that is already endangered.

> acres　　　common　　　species　　　strategies　　　victims

　オーストラリアには、コアラが４万匹から８万匹いるとされるが、個体数が減少し、International Union for Conservation of Nature 国際自然保護連合は、絶滅の危険のある「危急種」に指定している。コアラの生息数減に歯止めをかけるため、2018年にはニューサウスウエールズ州の森林地帯を保護区や国立公園に指定する「コアラ戦略」を発表している。
　しかし、2019年９月以降、東部ニューサウスウエールズ州では、270万ヘクタール以上の森林が焼失し、720棟以上の建物が被害を受けた。温暖化や気候変動により降雨不足のため火災が拡大したのが要因とされる。12月には、オーストラリアSBS放送が、森林火災で2000匹以上のコアラが死んだのではないかと報じた。
　2019年11月下旬までにブラジル国内で起きた森林火災は、18万件を超え、その６割以上がアマゾン川岸に集中した。野焼きの火の延焼が一因だと言われている。１年間に違法伐採や火災などで失われたアマゾンの森林面積は、日本の青森県に匹敵すると言われている。世界の環境保護団体は、アマゾンを「地球の肺」と訴えている。アマゾンの土はやせているため、牧草や農作物の育ちが悪い。農業や牛を飼っている人たちは、肥料が買えずに、代わりに灰を得るため開墾後も野焼きを繰り返している。

Reading

15

Saving the Fire Victims Who Cannot Flee: Australia's Koalas

The plight of dozens of animals being treated for burned paws and singed fur is raising fears about climate change and the future of the species.

MELBOURNE, Australia — The victims were carried in one by one, their paws burned and fur singed, suffering from dehydration and fear. Their caretakers bandaged their wounds, swaddled them and laid them in baskets with the only thing that was familiar — the leaves of a eucalyptus tree.

16

As catastrophic fires have burned more than two million acres in Australia, dozens of koalas have been rescued from smoldering trees and ashen ground. The animals, already threatened as a species before these latest blazes ravaged a crucial habitat, are being treated in rescue centers, and at least one private home, along the country's east coast.

"They are terrified," said Cheyne Flanagan, the clinical director of the Koala Hospital, in Port Macquarie, the only facility of its kind in the world. She added that what was happening to the koalas was "a national tragedy."

Officials at the hospital began warning weeks ago, when the fires first ignited around Port Macquarie, 250 miles north of Sydney, that hundreds of koalas may have been "incinerated."

17

The plight of the koala — a national symbol of Australia — has raised questions among conservationists and scientists about what it will take to preserve biodiversity in a country increasingly prone to intense fire, extreme heat and water scarcity, and which already has among the highest rates of species extinction in the world.

While koalas have evolved to exist alongside wildfires, the animals are facing new threats not just from climate change but also from human development, which has dislocated local populations, impairing their ability to survive fires. In some

Flee：逃げる

plight：窮状

paws：手足

species：種（としてのコア ラ）

dehydration：脱水症

swaddled ～：～を布で包 んだ

acres：エーカー《1エーカ ーは約4,000m²》

ravaged ～：～を荒廃させた

habitat：生息環境

clinical director：臨床部長 ・院長

warning ～：～と警報を発 する《目的語は that 以下》

incinerated：焼却処分され る

conservationists：環境保護 活動家

biodiversity：生物多種多様 性

prone to ～：～の傾向がある

which already has among the highest rates of species extinction：オー ストラリアは既に絶滅種の 比率が最も高い国だ《have among ～は be among ～の 変形》

exist alongside ～：～と共 存する

dislocated local populations：地元住民を 立ち退かせた《コアラを 指す》

impairing ～：～を弱める

regions, scientists say, koalas' numbers have declined by up
30 to 80 percent, though it is difficult to know how many remain
across Australia.

"We have these unique animals not found anywhere else
on this planet, and we're killing them," Ms. Flanagan said.
"This is a big wake-up call."

35 The animal distress goes beyond koalas. Recently, tens of
thousands of bats plummeted from the sky in temperatures
exceeding 107 degrees Fahrenheit in northern Australia.
Kangaroos, parched by drought, decimated the grapes on
a vineyard in Canberra. And waterfowl in the Macquarie
40 Marshes, a wildlife haven in northwest New South Wales,
have been affected by a fire in their habitat.

Koalas, unlike kangaroos, birds or snakes, do not flee from
fires, but instead scale trees to the canopy, where they can curl
themselves into a ball for protection and wait for the danger to
45 pass.

But during high-intensity fires, such as those that have
burned in recent weeks, the animals, conservationists say,
are far less likely to survive. Even if the fire itself does not
reach the tree canopy, the animals may overheat and fall to the
50 ground, where they can be burned to death.

The New York Times, November 14, 2019

by up to ～：最高～ほど
《by は程度を表す》

wake-up call：警鐘

plummeted：まっすぐに落
ちた

Fahrenheit：（温度を示す）
華氏《(F－32)×$\frac{5}{9}$＝C》
107F＝42C

parched by drought：干ば
つで喉がからからに乾いて

decimated ～：～を台無し
にした

Macquarie Marshes：マッ
コーリー湿地

wildlife haven：野生生物
保護区

canopy：樹冠

far less likely to ～：ほと
んど～しそうにない

Exercises

Multiple Choice

次の1〜3の英文の質問に答え、4〜5の英文を完成させるために、a〜dの中から最も適切なものを1つ選びなさい。

1. Most animals flee fires, but which do not depart at the first sign?

    a. Kangaroos.

    b. Snakes.

    c. Koalas.

    d. Orangutans.

2. What percentage of koalas have disappeared from Australia?

    a. 8%.   **c.** 48%.

    b. 18%.   **d.** 80%.

3. What item were injured koalas bandaged in and comforted by?

    a. Eucalyptus leaves.

    b. Baskets.

    c. Rescuers.

    d. Fur.

4. The many massive fires in Australia are an indication of

    a. overcrowding in the cities.

    b. tree-cutting throughout the country.

    c. bats invading the woods.

    d. climate change affecting the country.

5. The koala is described as

    a. unable to eat grapes.

    b. a national symbol.

    c. able to deal with fires.

    d. all of the above.

本文の内容に合致するものに T（True）、合致しないものに F（False）をつけなさい。

(　　) **1.** Scientists believe that in high intensity fires animals are likely to not survive.

(　　) **2.** Growth in Australia's human development is relevant to the displacement of koalas.

(　　) **3.** Many citizens of Australia are concerned about the future of koalas.

(　　) **4.** Koalas are native to several other countries.

(　　) **5.** Australia already has the highest level of species extinction.

Vocabulary

次の英文は、the Japan Times に掲載された *Coronavirus outbreak's silver lining for climate crisis likely to fade*『コロナウイルス発生は、薄れて行きそうな気候変動危機への明るい見通しだ』の記事の一部です。下の語群から最も適切なものを１つ選び、(　　) 内に記入しなさい。

Economic shock waves from the coronavirus outbreak have curbed (　　　　) pollution from China and beyond, but hopes for (　　　　) benefits from the slowdown are likely to be dashed quickly, experts say.

As governments prepare to spend their way out of the crisis, including with large infrastructure projects, global (　　　　) concerns will be little more than an afterthought, dwarfed by a drive to (　　　　) up a stuttering world economy, they say.

In the four weeks up to March 1, China's discharge of carbon dioxide (　　　　) 200 million tons, or 25 percent, compared to the same period last year, according to the Center for Research on Energy and Clean Air (CREA)- (　　　　) to annual carbon dioxide emissions from Argentina, Egypt or Vietnam.

As the country's economy (　　　　) to a crawl, coal consumption at power plants in China declined by 36 percent, and the use of oil at refineries by nearly as much.

"When you turn off the global fossil fuel economy, greenhouse gas emissions go down, air quality (　　　　)," said Jon Erickson. But any climate silver lining will be short-lived, experts warn.

carbon	climate	equivalent	fell
improves	prop	slowed	warming

4

● 上流階級育ちの坊ちゃんの中身のない自信に気をつけろ

英国オックスフォード大学での卒業式後の新卒業生たち。出身高校によって進むべき
将来が異なるのか？　　　　　　　　　　　　　　Photo: ロイター／アフロ

Before you read

1. What do you think the article will be about?

   この記事は何の話題についてだと思いますか？

2. What do you know about posh boys?

   上流階級育ちの坊ちゃんについて何か知っていますか？

次の１〜５の語の説明として最も近いものをa〜eから１つ選び、（　　）内に記入しなさい。

1. hollow	（　　）		**a.**	insistence
2. assertiveness	（　　）		**b.**	empty or baseless
3. slickness	（　　）		**c.**	run away
4. scurry	（　　）		**d.**	brutal honesty
5. bluntness	（　　）		**e.**	superficial confidence

次の英文は記事の要約です。下の語群から最も適切な語を１つ選び、（　　）内に記入しなさい。

20

The economic and political dominance of the privately-educated
(　　　　　　) in Britain. Even if they have only average intelligence,
their confidence and social (　　　　　　) bring them huge advantages.
Overconfidence is known to be a (　　　　　　) of errors and failures. But an
expensive education and posh (　　　　　) still give these people (　　　　　)
influence over politics, law and banking.

accent　　connections　　disproportionate　　persists　　source

　　18世紀後半に誕生したイギリスの階級は、産業革命の中から生まれた社会構造の変革だった。Upper Class 上流階級、Middle Class 中流階級、Working Class 労働者階級の３階級に分かれている。その後、中流階級にも upper middle class 上位中流階級、middle middle class 中位中流階級、lower middle class 下位中流階級に細分化され、５つの階級に分かれている。中には、７つの階級に分類する学者もいる。上流階級は、王族・貴族で構成され、上位中流階級は、医師、弁護士、官僚、軍人、中位中流が国会議員、企業経営者、会社重役、新聞記者、教師、警部、下位中流階級に不動産屋、写真家、銀行員、秘書、警官に当てはめることができる。労働者階級は、バスの運転手、土木作業員、日雇い労働者などの肉体労働者をさす。
　　現代のイギリスには、法的に制度化された階級はないが、人々の生活や意識の中に階級社会はしっかりと存在している。階級間には積極的な交流はなく、学校、購読新聞、使う英語の単語・アクセントなどが違う。所得や貯蓄、住宅資産などの経済、社会的紐帯の数と状況などの社会関係、美術館やコンサートへ行くなどの高尚な文化が階級格差を示している。上位中流階級は、社会的ネットワークに恵まれている。

Reading

21

Beware the posh boy's hollow self-confidence

We can't improve social mobility until we stop trusting in a firm handshake and cut-glass accent

Sixty years ago at Cambridge, Alan Bennet encountered public school boys for the first time. "I was appalled," he remembered, "they were loud, self-confident and all seemed to know one another." In 2011, at Oxford, I had the same
5 reaction. This time they were all wearing tracksuits but the extraordinary levels of self-confidence were just as Bennet had recorded. Nothing had changed.

22

A study reported in *The Times* yesterday proves the bleedin' obvious; poshness breeds confidence. The higher
10 your perception of your social class, the more confident you're likely to be. Depressingly, the researchers then showed that confidence is an indicator of success, which in turn is an indicator of high social class, which is an indicator of confidence. You get the picture; it's a vicious circle.

15 A 2016 report by the Sutton Trust found that sociability, confidence and assertiveness are "particularly beneficial for career success". People with those traits are 25 per cent more likely to be in jobs that pay more than £40,000 a year. The same study found that those characteristics were overwhelmingly
20 associated with people from affluent backgrounds. And not only will a private education land you a better paying job, it'll land you a more powerful job too. The privately educated are disproportionately represented in roles with greater opportunities for decision-making and leadership.

23
25 When you pay £30,000 a year to send your child to private school you're mainly buying confidence. You get good grades, sure (about 50 per cent of privately educated kids get As and A*s at A level), but the confidence takes you even further. A privately educated man leaving university with the same
30 degree as a state-educated man will go on to earn 7 to 15 per

posh：上流階級育ちの
hollow：中身のない

social mobility：社会的流動性

cut-glass accent：上流階級のような発音

public school：パブリックスクール《英国では中高一貫の私立学校》

The Times：タイムズ《英国で1785年に創刊された世界最古の日刊新聞；政治的傾向は中道右派》

bleedin' obvious：非常に明白なこと《ロンドン下町言葉》

You get the picture：話が見えただろう

vicious circle：悪循環

Sutton Trust：サットントラスト《英国の教育慈善団体》

assertiveness：自己主張

traits：特徴・特質

from affluent backgrounds：裕福な環境で育った

private education：（小中高の）私教育《公教育は state education》

land 〜 …：〜を…に連れていく

powerful job：力をふるえる仕事

As and A*s at A level：大学入試資格を得るAレベルでの（成績の）優（A）や秀（S）

cent more.

In the five years since I left university I've observed this phenomenon myself. My privately educated contemporaries are much more likely to be working in high-status careers like law, banking or journalism. Many of my state-educated friends work in service jobs or have moved back to their home towns. I'm sure the lack of confidence to have a go in highly competitive industries is a factor.

As a country we're as awed by posh confidence as we've ever been; the slickness of the hair, the firmness of the handshake. A glance at our political leaders confirms this. The sackings and political disasters endured by Boris Johnson might have sent a less assertive man scurrying back to his burrow. Not so Boris; his ironclad Etonian confidence is propelling him towards the leadership of the Conservative Party.

If posh confidence isn't going away, it's up to us to wean ourselves off the habit of equating confidence with ability. After all, the consequences could be terrible. The researchers from the first study I quoted point out with engaging bluntness that "overconfidence is believed to be a significant underlying cause for many catastrophes, such as wars, strikes, litigation, entrepreneurial failures, and stock market bubbles". And you thought Boris Johnson was bad.

The Times, May 22, 2019

confirm 〜：〜を裏付ける

Boris Johnson：ボリス・ジョンソン英国現首相

burrow：隠れ穴、避難場所

Etonian：イートン校卒業生の《英国の超名門パブリックスクール》

propelling 〜 towards …：〜を…へ駆り立てる

Conservative Party：保守党《英国２大政党の１つ》

up to us：私たち次第だ

wean ourselves off 〜：〜を止める

equating 〜 with …：〜と…を同一視する

with engaging bluntness：ひときわ目立つほどの無愛想さで

underlying cause：根本原因

litigation：訴訟

entrepreneurial：起（企）業家の

stock market：証券市場

And you thought 〜：さあ、これで〜と思っただろう

Exercises

次の１～５の英文を完成させるために、 a～dの中から最も適切なものを１つ選びなさい。

1. This article states that
   a. those from public schools will earn 7 to 15% less than students from state schools.
   b. those from a state school will earn 7 to 15% more than the public school students.
   c. confidence acquired from the home and public school environment may enable students to raise their salary earning power.
   d. there is little relationship between the kind of schooling received and confidence and success in the business world.

2. The qualities attributed to "posh boys" include
   a. sociability.
   b. assertiveness.
   c. confidence.
   d. all of the above.

3. By "vicious circle", the author means that
   a. public school students have qualities necessary for success reinforced by their affluent family, teachers, and fellow students.
   b. intelligence, rather than schooling, affects one's job and salary.
   c. Boris Johnson lacks the proper credentials to be a "posh boy."
   d. confidence and sociability are less important in today's world.

4. Overconfidence can have negative consequences such as
   a. business success.
   b. exceptional ability.
   c. economic problems.
   d. lack of ambition.

5. The author of this article feels
   a. Johnson is capable but lacks confidence.
   b. poshness has become a barrier to becoming prime minister.
   c. we need to stop trusting in the abilities of the posh.
   d. we are fortunate to have politicians from elite backgrounds.

本文の内容に合致するものに T（True）、合致しないものに F（False）をつけなさい。

(   ) **1.** High social class seems to be determined by family background, the school attended, and the personality traits acquired.

(   ) **2.** Jobs worked by state school graduates tend to be lower paying and less valued.

(   ) **3.** A firm handshake has little influence on employment success.

(   ) **4.** You would probably find more lawyers attended public schools.

(   ) **5.** According to this article in certain situations tracksuits are seemingly worn by public school students.

Vocabulary

次の 1 ～ 6 は、「posh」を使用している英文です。下の語群から 1 つ選び、(   ) 内に記入しなさい。

1. She celebrated her birthday at the (   ) hotel in town.

2. She talks so (   ) she sounds like the Queen.

3. She will be getting all (   ) up for a banquet.

4. She is thinking of (   ) up her apartment with new curtains.

5. She drives a Rolls-Royce? You can't get (   ) than that.

6. (   ) has become a path to promotion.

posh	poshed	posher
poshest	poshing	poshness

5

● ノート型パソコンのリサイクルでの代償：タイで有毒ガスが

タイ国内の電子廃棄物処理工場で作業する外国人労働者
Photo: The New York Times ／ Redux ／アフロ

Before you read

Kingdom of Thailand
タイ王国

面積　514,000km²（日本の約1.4倍）（世界50位）
人口　68,910,000人（世界20位）
公用語　タイ語
首都　バンコク
民族　タイ族　75%
　　　華人　　14%
　　　マレー系、インド系、モン族、カレン族
宗教　仏教　94%
　　　イスラム教　5%
GDP　4,872億ドル（世界26位）
　　　1人当たり GDP　7,187ドル（世界84位）
通貨　バーツ
政体　立憲君主制
識字率　95%

次の１〜５の語の説明として最も近いものをａ〜ｅから１つ選び、（　）内に記入しなさい。

1.	crouch	（　　）	**a.**	rebuff
2.	repel	（　　）	**b.**	material from used computers or phones
3.	salvage	（　　）	**c.**	sit or bend down close to the ground
4.	e-waste	（　　）	**d.**	well-intentioned
5.	virtuous	（　　）	**e.**	collect for recycling

Summary

次の英文は記事の要約です。下の語群から最も適切な語を１つ選び、（　）内に記入しなさい。

26

（　　　　　） e-waste seems like a good idea. But it is dirty and (　　　　　) dangerous. Conscious of the (　　　　　), China and Thailand stopped importing used computers and phones. But the work still goes on in the latter, sometimes (　　　　　). One Chinese firm employs low-paid laborers there, many of them (　　　　　), to do this hazardous work with little protection.

> illegal   potentially   recycling   risks   secretly

　1989年に有害廃棄物の国際的な移動を規制する「バーゼル条約」が採択された。さらに、2021年から汚れたプラスティックごみが対象に加わることが決まった。

　タイの経済も堅調に推移し、工業化や都市化が進む反面、環境公害問題が引き起こされている。有害廃棄物である廃有機溶剤の適正処理が課題となり、タイ政府の環境セクターが改善に積極的に取り組んでいる。

　しかし、2020年３月に新型コロナウイルスの感染防止対策として「非常事態」が宣言され、飲食店は、持ち帰りと宅配での営業のみとなり、プラスティック製の容器、スプーン等が多用され、１日当たりのプラスティックごみ発生量が想定より約15％も増加したと言われている。タイを含む東南アジアは、屋台文化が浸透していて、使い捨てプラスティック製品の大量消費地とされている。ASEAN の「バンコク宣言」が採択され、レジ袋の利用制限が行われている。

　日本でもごみ減量のため、reduce 発生抑制、reuse 再使用、recycle 再生利用の３Ｒの推進運動が行われている。2017年末に中国がプラスティックゴミ輸入を禁止したが、スウェーデンでは1904年以来115年以上も年間80万トンのゴミを近隣諸国から輸入している。自国のゴミも含めて埋め立て処理されるのはたった１％、残りの99％中半分がリサイクル、半分は焼却され、電力に転換されている。

Reading

27

The Price of Recycling Old Laptops: Toxic Fumes in Thailand's Lungs

    KOH KHANUN, Thailand — Crouched on the ground in a dimly lit factory, the women picked through the discarded innards of the modern world: batteries, circuit boards and bundles of wires.

5   They broke down the scrap — known as e-waste — with hammers and raw hands. Men, some with faces wrapped in rags to repel the fumes, shoveled the refuse into a clanking machine that salvages usable metal.

28

    As they toiled, smoke spewed over nearby villages and
10 farms. Residents have no idea what is in the smoke: plastic, metal, who knows? All they know is that it stinks and they feel sick.

    The factory, New Sky Metal, is part of a thriving e-waste industry across Southeast Asia, born of China's decision
15 to stop accepting the world's electronic refuse, which was poisoning its land and people. Thailand in particular has become a center of the industry even as activists push back and its government wrestles to balance competing interests of public safety with the profits to be made from the lucrative
20 trade.

29

    Last year, Thailand banned the import of foreign e-waste. Yet new factories are opening across the country, and tons of e-waste are being processed, environmental monitors and industry experts say.

25   "E-waste has to go somewhere," said Jim Puckett, the executive director of the Basel Action Network, which campaigns against trash dumping in poor countries, "and the Chinese are simply moving their entire operations to Southeast Asia."

30   "The only way to make money is to get huge volume with cheap, illegal labor and pollute the hell out of the environment,"

Price：代償

Laptops：ノート型パソコン

Toxic Fumes：有毒ガス

KOH KHANUN：カヌン島

picked through 〜：〜を丹念に調べた

discarded：捨てられた

circuit boards：回路基板

e-waste：電子廃棄物

refuse：廃物、ごみ

spewed over 〜：〜の上に向かって吐き出た

stinks：悪臭を放つ

poisoning 〜：〜を汚染する

push back：反対する

competing interest of public safety with 〜：〜と競合する公共の安全利益

environmental monitors：環境管理者

executive director：事務局長

trash dumping：ごみの投げ捨て

get huge volume with cheap, illegal labor：安い賃金で不法労働させて大量生産する

the hell out of：徹底的に、ひどく

he added.

Each year, 50 million tons of electronic waste are produced globally, according to the United Nations, as consumers grow
35 accustomed to throwing away last year's model and acquiring the next new thing.

The notion of recycling these gadgets sounds virtuous: an infinite loop of technological utility.

But it is dirty and dangerous work to extract the tiny
40 quantities of precious metals — like gold, silver and copper — from castoff phones, computers and televisions.

For years, China took in much of the world's electronic refuse. Then in 2018, Beijing closed its borders to foreign e-waste. Thailand and other countries in Southeast Asia —
45 with their lax enforcement of environmental laws, easily exploited labor force and cozy nexus between business and government — saw an opportunity.

In June of last year, the Thai Ministry of Industry announced with great fanfare the ban on foreign e-waste.
50 The police made a series of high-profile raids on at least 10 factories, including New Sky Metal.

"New Sky is closed now, totally closed," Yutthana Poolpipat, the head of the Laem Chabang Port customs bureau, said in September. "There is no electronic waste coming into
55 Thailand, zero."

But a recent visit to the hamlet of Koh Khanun showed that the factory was still up and running, as are many others, a reflection of the weak regulatory system and corruption that has tainted the country.

The New York Times, December 8, 2019

virtuous：道徳にかなった

extract 〜 from …：…から〜を取り出す

castoff：廃棄処分された

lax enforcement：緩い適用

cozy nexus：結託した結びつき、癒着

made raids on 〜：急襲した、手入れを行った

high-profile：人目を惹く

Laem Chabang Port：レムチャバン港《タイ中部にある同国を代表する港湾》

customs bureau：関税局

up and running：立ち上がって稼働している

reflection of 〜：〜を反映するもの

regulatory system：規制制度

corruption：汚職

tainted 〜：〜を汚染してきた

Exercises

Multiple Choice
次の1〜5の英文を完成させるために、a〜dの中から最も適切なものを1つ選びなさい。

1. The Chinese stopped recycling electronic scrap because
   - **a.** it was a lucrative trade.
   - **b.** it was employing too many people.
   - **c.** it produced lower profits.
   - **d.** it was poisoning their land.

2. Thailand's e-waste plants are dangerous because of
   - **a.** smoke pouring over villages and farms.
   - **b.** toxic fumes making people sick.
   - **c.** the conditions in which people work.
   - **d.** all of the above.

3. Corruption in the government of Thailand has
   - **a.** allowed a few factories to continue operating.
   - **b.** enabled the removal of all factories of e-waste.
   - **c.** led to strictly enforced environmental laws.
   - **d.** improved the air quality in places like Koh Khanun.

4. The Thai government
   - **a.** denies any connection between e-waste and sickness.
   - **b.** acknowledges the import of cheap illegal workers.
   - **c.** openly welcomes any industry that makes large profits.
   - **d.** officially bans the import of foreign e-waste.

5. Jim Puckett seems to be
   - **a.** uninterested in the factories in Thailand.
   - **b.** recommending the use of cheap illegal labor.
   - **c.** an owner of an e-waste business.
   - **d.** saying that it is difficult to control illegal e-waste industries.

本文の内容に合致するものに T (True)、合致しないものに F (False) をつけなさい。

(　　) **1.** Thailand banned the import of e-waste last year.

(　　) **2.** There has been a transfer of e-waste to poor countries in Southeast Asia.

(　　) **3.** The main motive for e-waste processing is probably how lucrative the work is.

(　　) **4.** The work is desirable and altruistic.

(　　) **5.** The innards of computers, phones, or televisions have not been proven to be poison or poisonous.

Vocabulary

　次 の 英文 は、the Japan Times に 掲載 さ れ た ”*Throwaway society: Rejecting a life consumed by plastic*’『使い捨て社会：プラスティックが消費生活を拒絶する』 の記事の 一部です。下の語群から最も適切な語を 1 つ選び、(　　　) 内に記入しなさい。

　Japan is (　　　　) for its use of disposable plastic. Elaborate but often (　　　　) food packaging is ubiquitous in supermarkets and convenience stores all over the country, and Japanese shoppers use an estimated 30 billion plastic shopping bags a year.

　Japan is the world's (　　　　)-biggest producer of plastic waste per capita behind the United States, and goes through around 9 million tons of plastic waste each year. Of that, more than 40 percent is (　　　　) plastic such as packaging and food containers.

　"Whether you go to a convenience store or a supermarket, you basically have (　　　　) option but to use disposable plastic," says Hiroaki Odachi, project leader of Greenpeace Japan's plastic campaign. "Whatever you buy, it comes (　　　　) in packaging.

　You don't need to spend long in Japan to notice how much single-use plastic there is, but is it really (　　　　) to avoid it? I decide to find out, and set myself a goal of not using any plastic that is designed to be (　　　　) away after a single use for a whole week.

disposable	impossible	infamous	no
second	thrown	unnecessary	wrapped

Unit 6

●他の人たちよりもずっと感染力が強い人たちがいる理由

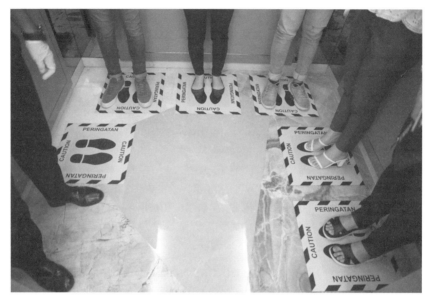

新型コロナウイルス感染流行でインドネシアではエレベーター内の立ち位置を指定

Photo: AP ／アフロ

Before you read

1〜7の「epidemic 疫病」に関連するものをa〜gの中から1つ選び、（　　　）内に記入しなさい。

1. plague　ペスト　　　　　　　　（　　）　　**a.** Spanish influenza
2. Spanish Flu　スペイン風邪　　（　　）　　**b.** vaccination
3. tuberculosis　結核　　　　　　（　　）　　**c.** Covid-19
4. smallpox　天然痘　　　　　　　（　　）　　**d.** found in soil
5. tetanus　破傷風　　　　　　　　（　　）　　**e.** Black Death
6. coronavirus　コロナウイルス　（　　）　　**f.** Robert Koch
7. cholera　コレラ　　　　　　　　（　　）　　**g.** contaminated water

次の1～5の語句の説明として最も近いものをa～eから1つ選び、（　　）内に記入しなさい。

1. infectious （　　） a. vulnerable
2. at play （　　） b. sudden and expansive emergence
3. misattribute （　　） c. contributory or relevant
4. outbreak （　　） d. connect falsely
5. susceptible （　　） e. likely to pass on to someone else

Summary

次の英文は記事の要約です。下の語群から最も適切な語を1つ選び、（　　）内に記入しなさい。

32

Some people seem to spread illnesses more (　　　　　) than others. In Hong Kong, a (　　　　　) small number transmitted SARS to a relatively large number. The (　　　　　) was true of Ebola in Africa. (　　　　　), most MERS-sufferers in Korea did not pass on the disease. Understanding the reasons for the differences is complex, involving (　　　　　) study of matters such as social behavior.

close   conversely   easily   relatively   same

　2019年11月17日に中華人民共和国湖北省出身の男性が新型コロナウイルスの最初の症例だったと South China Morning Post が報じている。しかし、実際には11月22日に湖北省武漢市で「原因不明のウイルス性肺炎」として最初の症例が確認された。武漢市内の武漢華南海鮮卸売市場で同定され、それ以降、武漢市内から中国大陸へ感染が広がり、187以上の国々に感染が広がった。20年8月10日現在感染者数2,040万人を上回り、死亡者数74.4万、回復者数1,263万である。世界各国の主要都市で都市封鎖や移動制限の Lockdown が実施され、社会的・経済的に大きな損益を及ぼしている。

　日本では新型コロナウイルスと呼んでいるが、正式には SARS-CoV-2（Severe acute respiratory syndrome coronavirus version 2）と命名された。しかし欧米のメディアでは、Covid-19を使っている。中国浙江省舟山市のコウモリから発見された SARS ウイルスとの類似度を持つと言われている。コロナウイルスには複数の型があり、武漢市の大流行はL型で全体の7割を占める。S型は全体の3割でコウモリ由来のウイルスに近い。

　日本でも20年4月17日に全国に「緊急事態宣言」が出され、手洗いの徹底、マスク着用、social distancing, 密接・密閉・密集の3密の回避を徹する「新しい生活様式」が促されている。その後、5月25日をもって日本全国で「緊急事態宣言」が解除された。しかし、8月12日の全国の感染者数が5万人を超えた。

33

Why Are Some People So Much More Infectious Than Others?

Solving the mystery of "superspreaders" could help control the coronavirus pandemic.

superspreaders：スーパー・スプレッダー、超感染拡大者

Distinguishing between those who are more infectious and those less infectious could make an enormous difference in the ease and speed with which an outbreak is contained, said Jon Zelner, an epidemiologist at the University of Michigan.
5 If the infected person is a superspreader, contact tracing is especially important. But if the infected person is the opposite of a superspreader, someone who for whatever reason does not transmit the virus, contact tracing can be a wasted effort.

Distinguishing between 〜 and …：〜と…との違いが分かる

make a difference in 〜：〜において効果がある

ease：容易さ

contained：阻止される

epidemiologist：疫学者、伝染病学者

contact tracing：接触者追跡

34

"The tricky part is that we don't necessarily know who 10 those people are," Dr. Zelner said.

tricky：扱いにくい

Two factors are at play, said Martina Morris, emeritus professor of statistics and sociology at the University of Washington.

at play：登場する

emeritus professor：名誉教授

statistics：統計学

"There has to be a link between people in order to transmit 15 an infection," she said. But, she added, a link "is necessary but not sufficient." The second factor is how infectious a person is. "We almost never have independent data on those two things," Dr. Morris said.

independent：独自の

She pointed out that it can be easy to misattribute multiple 20 infections to an individual — possibly exposing the person to public attack — when the spread has nothing to do with the person's infectiousness.

misattribute 〜 to …：誤って〜を…のせいにする

multiple infections：多重感染

public attack：公然たる非難

Yet there do seem to be situations in which a few individuals spark large outbreaks.

do seem：《動詞の強調》

25 In 2003 during the SARS outbreak, the first patient in Hong Kong appears to have infected at least 125 others. Other superspreading events involved 180 people in a housing complex in Hong Kong and another 22 people on a jet from Hong Kong to Beijing.

SARS：サーズ（重症急性呼吸器症候群）

housing complex：団地

30   In the Ebola outbreak in Africa between 2014 and 2016, 61 percent of infections were traced to just 3 percent of infected people.

    At the other end of the bell curve of infectiousness are infected people who do not seem to infect others. During the
35 MERS outbreak in South Korea, 89 percent of patients did not appear to transmit the disease.

    In the Covid-19 pandemic, there is a striking example from the far end of uninfectious — a couple in Illinois.

    On Jan. 23 the wife, who had returned from a visit
40 to Wuhan, became the first laboratory-confirmed case of Covid-19 in the state. On Jan. 30, her husband was infected. It was the first known person-to-person transmission in the United States.

    Both husband and wife became gravely ill and were
45 hospitalized. Both recovered. State public health officials traced their contacts — 372 people, including 195 health care workers. Not a single one became infected.

    Dr. Jennifer Layden, chief medical officer for the Chicago Department of Public Health, said the remarkable lack of
50 spread probably arose from several factors. Where were the couple in the course of their infection when they came into contact with those other people? Were they sneezing or coughing? How close were the contacts? Were the people they interacted with simply less susceptible to infections?

The New York Times, April 12, 2020

Ebola：エボラ出血熱

bell curve：ベル（釣鐘）型曲線

are infected people：《副詞句の強調による倒置：infected people are》

MERS：マーズ（中東呼吸器症候群）

Covid-19：新型コロナウイルス感染症

uninfectious：非感染症の、感染を引き起こすことのできない

Wuhan：武漢

laboratory-confirmed：検査で確認された

public health officials：公衆衛生当局

chief medical officer：医務部長

Where：どの段階に

in the course of ～：～の過程の

sneezing：＜しゃみする

close：濃厚な、近づいて

interacted with ～：～と関わった

susceptible to ～：～にかかり易い、～に影響を受ける

Exercises

次の１〜３の英文の質問に答え、４〜５の英文を完成させるために、ａ〜ｄの中から最も適切なものを１つ選びなさい。

1. What makes contact tracing both important and a waste of time?

   a. Incomplete calculations of data.
   b. Finding a superspreader.
   c. Finding an infected person who does not spread the virus.
   d. None of the above.

2. What percentage of Ebola infections came from what percentage of infected people?

   a. 3% from 61% of infected people.
   b. 19% from 3% of infected people.
   c. 61% from 29% of infected people.
   d. 61% from 3% of infected people.

3. A woman returning from Wuhan infected her husband. How many others were infected by them?

   a. Only two.
   b. 372 people.
   c. None.
   d. There is no data on their contacts.

4. During the SARS outbreak, the first person in Hong Kong infected

   a. 22 people.
   b. 80 people.
   c. 125 people.
   d. 180 people.

5. Possible reasons for non-infection of others from the first woman returning from Wuhan are

   a. lack of close the contacts with the people.
   b. absence of coughs and sneezes when meeting their contact.
   c. the low susceptible of the contacts themselves.
   d. all of the above.

本文の内容に合致するものに T（True）、合致しないものに F（False）をつけなさい。

(   ) **1.** In South Korea in the MERS epidemic, 89% of the people tested were found not to transmit the disease.

(   ) **2.** The "superspreader" mystery being solved might help control the Covid-19 problem.

(   ) **3.** People can become infected even while flying on a plane.

(   ) **4.** Finding out who is more infectious is not relevant to the outbreak.

(   ) **5.** This article mentions patients who unfortunately died.

Vocabulary

次の英文は、the New York Times に掲載された *How to Save Black and Hispanic Lives in a Pandemic*『世界的に広がっている伝染病から黒人とヒスパニック系の人々を救う方法』の記事の一部です。下の語群から最も適切な語を１つ選び、（　　　）内に記入しなさい。

Across the United States, black and Hispanic people suffer disproportionately from (　　　　　), poor health care and (　　　　) diseases like diabetes, hypertension and asthma.

As the pandemic continues, it is crucial that local and state health departments across the country report data on how the coronavirus is (　　　　) people by (　　　　) and also by gender and age.

The racial disparities may be predictable, but they are (　　　　) nonetheless. Public health experts say there are actions that states and cities can take right now to help (　　　　) lives. Doing so would help protect all vulnerable people.

The country's response to the pandemic remains (　　　　) by medical supply shortages. As masks, gloves and other protective equipment become more available, it is clear that all essential workers require them, not just emergency and medical personnel. That includes janitors, home health aides, delivery people, grocery and farm workers and sanitation workers. In New York City, as in many cities, much of the municipal (　　　　) force is black or Hispanic.

affecting	chronic	hampered	poverty
race	save	tragic	work

●疫病の渦中で必要なのはフランスではペイストリーとワイン、米国ではゴルフと銃

新型コロナウイルス感染流行でもフランスは飲食店再開。前を通り過ぎる人たちはマスクを着用

Photo: ロイター／アフロ

Before you read

1. What do you think the article will be about?

   この記事は何の話題についてだと思いますか？

2. What is essential for you in the middle of an epidemic?

   疫病の渦中であなたにとって必要なものは何ですか？

次の１〜５の語句の説明として最も近いものをa〜eから１つ選び、（　）内に記入しなさい。

1. bid   （　　）   **a.** collapse into chaos
2. exempt   （　　）   **b.** illness
3. a good deal of   （　　）   **c.** attempt
4. ailment   （　　）   **d.** excepted
5. breakdown   （　　）   **e.** much

次の英文は記事の要約です。下の語群から最も適切な語を１つ選び、（　）内に記入しなさい。

38

In response to the novel coronavirus governments throughout the world
(　　　　　) business activity, while granting (　　　　　) to services
considered essential. But ideas about what is essential (　　　　　)
considerably. Guns and golf seem to be (　　　　) for many Americans.
Praying outside is important to Israelis. And (　　　　　), the French
prioritize wine and fine food.

exceptions   necessary   restricted   unsurprisingly   vary

　2020年３月25日、新型コロナウイルスの感染拡大防止のため、都知事が週末や夜間の不要不急の外出、飲食を伴う会合の自粛などを要請した。４月８日に７都府県を対象に『緊急事態宣言』が出され、17日には日本全国に拡大した。不要不急の外出などを控える自粛生活へと突入した。２月頃から、国民も「巣ごもり」姿勢を強めていた。

　５月８日に総務省が３月の家計調査を発表した。飲食関係では、長期保存可能な食品への買いだめ需要が高まり、パスタ（44.4％増）や即席めん（30.6％増）、チュウハイ・カクテル（22.8％増）が伸びた。しかし、自宅外での外食代（30.3％減）、飲酒代（53.5％減）が減少した。自宅での娯楽用としてのゲーム機は、165.8％も増え、2019年３月の消費額に比べて2.7倍になった。テレワークによる在宅勤務や動画配信サービスの需要増などで「インターネット接続料」も12.4％増加した。

　自宅用としてトイレットペーパー買いだめのため26.4％増、体温計75.6％と跳ね上がった。３密回避、「外出自粛」のため、映画、旅行、ガソリン、航空運賃、鉄道通勤・通学定期代などの消費が大幅に減少した。

Reading

39

What's essential? In France, pastry and wine – in the US, golf and guns

| Some activities reflect a national identity. |

The coronavirus pandemic is defining for the world what is "essential" and what things we really cannot do without, even though we might not need them for survival.

Authorities in many places are determining what shops
5 and services can remain open, in a bid to slow the spread of the virus.

Whether it is in Asia, Europe, Africa or the United States, there is general agreement – health care workers, law enforcement, utility workers, food production and
10 communications are generally exempt from lockdowns.

40

But some lists of exempted activities reflect a national identity, or the efforts of lobbyists.

In some US states, golf, guns and marijuana have been ruled essential, raising eyebrows and, in the case of guns, a
15 good deal of ire.

"Recent events clearly demonstrate that the process of designating 'essential services' is as much about culture as any legal-political reality about what is necessary to keep society functioning," said Christopher McKnight Nichols, associate
20 professor of history at Oregon State University, in the US.

Countries including India and US states are listing the information technology sector as essential.

The world's dependency on the internet has become even more apparent as countless people confined to their homes
25 communicate, stream movies and play games online to stave off cabin fever.

41

Several states where marijuana is legal, such as California and Washington, deemed pot shops and workers in the market's supply chain essential.
30 "Cannabis is a safe and effective treatment that millions

national identity：国民性

defining ～：～の意味を明らかにする

for the world：絶対に、断じて

do without ～：～無しです ます

Authorities：行政官庁

in a bid to ～：～の措置として

law enforcement：(警察などの) 法執行機関

utility workers：作業員

exempt from ～：～が適用されない、免除される

lobbyists：ロビイスト《ロビー活動とは、特定の主張を有する個人または団体が政府の政策に影響を及ぼすことを目的として行う詩的な政治活動》

ruled：規定される

raising eyebrows：人を驚かせる

ire：憤激（させる）

designating ～：～を指定する

stave off ～：～を回避する

cabin fever：ストレス

deemed ～ …：～を…と判断した

pot：マリファナ

Cannabis：大麻

of Americans rely on to maintain productive daily lives while suffering from diseases and ailments," Erik Altieri, executive director of the National Organisation for the Reform of Marijuana Laws, said.

35　Texas attorney general Ken Paxton issued a legal opinion saying emergency orders in his state cannot restrict gun sales.

"If you have a breakdown in society, well then our first line to defend ourselves is ourselves, so I think having a weapon is very important for your personal safety," Texas lieutenant 40　governor Dan Patrick told a radio interviewer.

In Arizona, governor Doug Ducey included golf courses on his list. Officials in Phoenix encouraged the city's 1.7 million residents to "get outside, get exercise and practice responsible social distancing" in golf courses, parks and trails.

45　In Europe, the current epicentre of the pandemic, Italy has the most stringent rules, with only essential businesses such as food shops and pharmacies remaining open.

The manufacturing sector was ordered shut down on Thursday, though factories that make needed products 50　like medical supplies will continue to operate after making conditions safer for employees.

In France, shops specialising in pastry, wine and cheese have been declared essential businesses.

In a nod to Israel's vibrant religious life, people can gather 55　for outdoor prayers, with a maximum of 10 worshippers standing two metres apart.

Aimee Huff, marketing professor at Oregon State University, specialising in consumer culture, said: "In times of uncertainty, institutions and practices that are central to the 60　cultural identities can become really important touchstones, material markers of certainty, comfort, and mechanisms to persist."

The Express & Star, March 19, 2020

---

ailments：（軽い）慢性病

National Organisation for the Reform of Marijuana Laws：マリファナ法改正を求める全国組織

attorney general：（州の）司法長官

restrict ～：～を制限する

breakdown：機能停止

lieutenant governor：州副知事

encouraged ～ to …：～に…すよう奨励した

trails：未舗装道路、小道、田舎道

epicentre：震源地

pharmacies：薬局

medical supplies：医療用品

In a nod to ～：～を考慮して

prayers：祈り

touchstones：試金石、基準《become の補語は touchstones, markers そして mechanisms の3つ》

markers：標識

mechanisms：仕組み

persist：存続する

Exercises

次の、1〜2の英文の質問に答え、3〜5の英文を完成させるために、a〜dの中から最も適切なものを1つ選びなさい。

1. While being in lockdown position, which essentials are somewhat surprising?

   a. Golfs, guns, and marijuana in parts of the US.
   b. The importance of the Internet and IT in India and the US.
   c. Food in various parts of Europe.
   d. Health care work around the world.

2. In what country would you see groups of 10 in prayer standing 2 metres apart?

   a. India.
   b. Pakistan.
   c. Israel.
   d. Myanmar.

3. For a long period during the Covid-19 pandemic in Italy

   a. shops were closed but large restaurants stayed open.
   b. all shops except grocery stores and pharmacies were closed.
   c. shops remained open but citizens had to stay home for many weeks.
   d. only the opera halls were closed.

4. The essential cultural necessities in France are

   a. cheese and rice.
   b. wine and bread.
   c. pastry and pasta.
   d. cheese, pastry and wine.

5. This article explains that

   a. in crises people desire things that are unfamiliar and exciting.
   b. different items allow people to feel comfortable in different cultures.
   c. scientists have found that people can exist without cultural foods and items.
   d. most people prioritize luxurious things in a crisis.

True or False

本文の内容に合致するものにＴ（True）、合致しないものにＦ（False）をつけなさい。

(   ) **1.** Some activities or items or food are considered necessary by citizens but they do not ensure their survival of Covid-19 virus.

(   ) **2.** Some items show national identity, like French emphasis on wine, cheese, and pastries.

(   ) **3.** Not everyone in the U.S. feels guns, golf, and marijuana are comforting items.

(   ) **4.** The Texas Attorney General is not in favor of guns and wants extra restrictions on gun sales.

(   ) **5.** Italy was forced into closing factories that make the medical supplies needed during a pandemic.

Vocabulary

次の１〜７は、「Coronavirus」に関する英文です。日本文に合わせて、適当な語を下の語群から１つ選び、（   ）内に記入しなさい。

1. 飲食を伴う宴会は控えて頂きますようお願いします。

We request that you (   ) from parties accompanied by eating and drinking.

2. 政府により、緊急事態宣言が出された。

A state of (   ) declaration is called by the government.

3. 特に不要不急の仕事の場合は、できるだけ在宅勤務をお願いします。

The authorities ask that people work from home as much as possible, especially if your work is considered (   ) and nonurgent.

4. 政府は、海外への渡航の自粛をお願いしています。

The government has now asked people here to refrain from travel (   ).

5. 新型コロナウイルスの感染拡大のため、2020年の東京オリンピックは延期になった。

Due to the spread of infection from the novel coronavirus, the 2020 Tokyo Olympics is (   ).

6. 自粛ムードは、経済にも影響している。

The air of (   ) has also had an effect on the economy.

7. 感染拡大で日経平均株価が下落する。

The Nikkei Stock Average goes down as the (   ) of contagion rises.

emergency	nonessential	overseas	postponed
refrain	self-restraint	spread	

•iPhone のはるか前に無線社会の基礎を築いた人たち

電池で科学技術の将来を築いたノーベル化学賞受賞者たち（写真は左から吉野さん、
グッドイナフ氏そしてウィッテンガム氏）　　　　Photo: TT News Agency ／アフロ

Before you read

Kingdom of Norway

Kingdom of Sweden

Finland

⊚Stockholm

Kingdom of Sweden
スウェーデン王国
面積　450,000km^2（日本の約1.2倍）（世界57位）
人口　10,220,000人（世界91位）
公用語　スウェーデン語
首都　ストックホルム
民族　スウェーデン人　85%
　　　フィンランド人　5％
宗教　キリスト教プロテスタント・ルター派80%
GDP　5,560億ドル（世界23位）
　　　1人当たり GDP　54,356ドル（世界12位）
通貨　スウェーデン・クローネ
政体　立憲君主制
識字率　99%

Words and Phrases

次の１〜５の語の説明として最も近いものをａ〜ｅから１つ選び、(　　)内に記入しなさい。

1. rechargeable 　(　　)
2. grid 　(　　)
3. sustainable 　(　　)
4. bulky 　(　　)
5. electrode 　(　　)

a. network
b. electrical conductor
c. able to be filled or activated again
d. using renewable resources
e. large and awkward

Summary

次の英文は記事の要約です。下の語群から最も適切な語を１つ選び、(　) 内に記入しなさい。

Compact lithium batteries are (　　　　　) in many of the electronic devices we use daily. Now the men who (　　　　) the technology, enabling Sony to develop batteries (　　　　), have been honored with a Nobel prize. Scientists Goodenough, Whittingham and Yoshino played key roles in (　　　　) the use of this super-light metal as an electrical (　　　　).

commercially　conductor　indispensable　pioneered　promoting

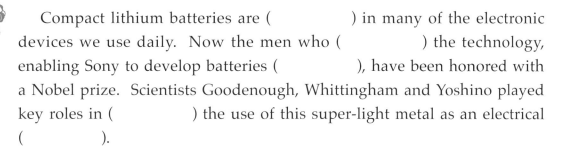

　2019年のノーベル化学賞は、吉野彰・旭化成名誉フェローと、テキサス大のジョン・グッドイナフ教授、ニューヨーク州立大のスタンリー・ウィッティンガム卓越教授に授与された。「リチウムイオン電池の開発」が授賞理由だ。リチウムイオン電池は、小型で軽量、高出力で、何度も充電でき、何度も使えるのが特徴である。スマートフォンやノートパソコンなどのモバイル機器や電気自動車などに広く使われ、現代社会の礎を築いたとされる。

　1970年代に、ウィッティンガム氏がプラス極に二硫化チタン、マイナス極に金属リチウムを使った電池を開発した。しかし、金属リチウムは他の物質と反応して発熱する危険があり、実用には至らなかった。80年代にグッドイナフ氏と東大助手として留学していた水島公一・東芝エグゼクティブフェローが、プラス極にコバルト酸リチウムを用いた電池を作製した。この電池の寿命はわずか数日だったが、約４ボルトの電圧を発生できた。

　1985年、吉野氏は電気を通すプラスティック「ポリアセチレン」をマイナス極に使い、プラス極にはグッドイナフ氏らのコバルト酸リチウムを用いた。さらに旭化成が開発した特殊な炭素繊維をマイナス極に使って、小型化する方法も開発し、現在のリチウムイオン電池の原型を完成させた。大容量で小型電池をさらに進めた次世代電池は、IT 機器、電気自動車、AI、ロボット、通信技術の発達の鍵を握るだろう。

Reading

They Laid Foundation For a Wireless Society

▌ Long Before iPhones ▌

The Royal Swedish Academy of Sciences awarded the 2019 Nobel Prize in Chemistry on Wednesday to three scientists who developed lithium-ion batteries, which have revolutionized portable electronics.

5　John B. Goodenough, M. Stanley Whittingham and Akira Yoshino will share the prize, which is worth about $900,000.

The three researchers' work in the 1970s and '80s led to the creation of powerful, lightweight and rechargeable batteries used in nearly every smartphone or laptop computer,
10　and in billions of cameras and power tools. Astronauts on the International Space Station rely on them, and engineers working on renewable energy grids often turn to them.

M. Stanley Whittingham, 77, a professor at Binghamton University, State University of New York, and one of the three
15　winners, said that he always hoped lithium-ion technology would grow, "but we never envisaged it growing this far. We never imagined it being ubiquitous in things like iPhones."

John B. Goodenough, 97, is a professor at the University of Texas at Austin. With the award he becomes the oldest
20　Nobel Prize winner, but is still active in research.

And Akira Yoshino, 71, is an honorary fellow for the Asahi Kasei Corporation in Tokyo and a professor at Meijo University in Nagoya, Japan. He said after the announcement that he was pleased that the technology could also help fight
25　climate change, calling lithium-ion batteries "suitable for a sustainable society."

The first rechargeable battery came about in 1859. These were made from lead-acid, and are still used to start gasoline- and diesel-powered vehicles today. But lead-acid batteries
30　were bulky and heavy. Nickel-cadmium batteries, which were less efficient but more compact, were invented in 1899.

Royal Swedish Academy of Science：スウェーデン王立科学アカデミー

lithium-ion batteries：リチウムイオン電池《イオンとは、電子の過剰あるいは欠損により電荷を帯びた原子または原子団》

electronics：電子機器

Akira Yoshino：吉野彰

rechargeable：再充電可能な

power tools：電動工具

renewable energy grids：再生可能なエネルギー供給網

Binghamton University：ビンガムトン大学《ニューヨーク州立大学を構成する大学の一つ》

envisaged ～：～を心に思い描く、想像する

Asahi Kasei Corporation：旭化成株式会社

Meijo University：名城大学

climate change：気候変動

sustainable society：持続可能な社会《国連の提唱する概念：将来の世代の欲求を損ねることなく、現在の世代の欲求も満足させる社会》

lead-acid：鉛酸

For many years, there were no major advancements in battery technology. But the Arab oil embargo of 1973 made many scientists realize the extent of society's dependence on
35 fossil fuels. Dr. Whittingham, who was working for Exxon at the time, began searching for improved ways to store energy from renewable sources and power electric cars.

He knew that lithium would make a good anode because it released electrons easily. It also had the advantage of being
40 the lightest metal. So Dr. Whittingham started looking for materials that had a high energy density and captured lithium-ions in the cathode — the side of your battery with the plus sign.

Dr. Whittingham discovered that titanium disulfide, which
45 had never been used in batteries before, had a molecular structure that let lithium-ions into small pockets. This resulted in the first functional lithium battery.

Dr. Goodenough, then at Oxford, predicted that lithium-ion batteries would have greater potential if the cathode were
50 made with a different material. He noticed that cobalt oxide was similar in structure to titanium disulfide.

Building from Dr. Goodenough's work, Dr. Yoshino, who was at the Asahi Kasei Corporation in Japan, then showed that more complicated carbon-based electrodes could house
55 lithium-ions in between their layers too.

These developments ultimately led to commercialization of the lithium-ion battery in 1991 by another Japanese electronics giant, Sony Corporation.

The New York Times International Edition, October 10, 2019

embargo：禁輸措置	
fossil fuels：化石燃料	
Exxon：エクソン《現在の エクソン・モービル：世界 最大の民間石油会社》	
power ～：～に動力・電力 を供給する	
anode：（電池の場合の）負 極	
high energy density：高エ ネルギー密度	
cathode：（電池の場合の） 正極	
plus sign：＋（プラス）記号	
titanium disulfide：二硫化 チタン	
molecular structure：分子 構造	
pockets：くぼみ、穴	
potential：電位	
cobalt oxide：酸化コバル ト	
Building from ～：～を発 展させて	
carbon-based electrodes： 炭素系電極	
house ～ in …：～を…に 収納する	
between their layers：層間	
electronics giant：電子工 業大手	

Exercises

Multiple Choice

次の１〜５の英文を完成させるために、 a〜d の中から最も適切なものを１つ選びなさい。

1. The three scientists who received the Nobel Prize in Chemistry
   - **a.** all came from the same country and worked together.
   - **b.** came from New York, Texas, and Japan but contributed to the same goal.
   - **c.** are receiving the prize at an early stage in their careers.
   - **d.** all went to the same university together.

2. The battery that could have a positive impact for a sustainable society is
   - **a.** the lithium-ion one.
   - **b.** the nickel-cadmium one.
   - **c.** the lead-acid one.
   - **d.** the environment-unfriendly one.

3. The oldest member of these Nobel Prize winners is
   - **a.** M. Stanley Whittingham.
   - **b.** Akira Yoshino.
   - **c.** John B. Goodenough.
   - **d.** unknown to us because their ages are not given in the article.

4. Lithium-ion is the
   - **a.** most comfortable battery.
   - **b.** bulkiest battery.
   - **c.** lightest battery.
   - **d.** oldest battery.

5. The lithium battery first became commercial in
   - **a.** the 1970s.
   - **b.** the 1980s.
   - **c.** the 1990s.
   - **d.** the early 2000s.

本文の内容に合致するものにＴ（True）、合致しないものにＦ（False）をつけなさい。

(　　) **1.** Dr. Goodenough is still active in his research.

(　　) **2.** The invention of Nickel-cadmium batteries transformed portable electronics.

(　　) **3.** iPhones are powered by lithium-ion batteries.

(　　) **4.** Even the scientists who won the Nobel Prize were amazed at the many adaptations of the lithium-ion battery.

(　　) **5.** In the early 1970s the world was not dependent on fossil fuels.

Vocabulary

次の英文は、読売新聞の The Japan News「えいご工房」に掲載された *Nobel awarded for developing battery*『電池開発にノーベル賞授与』の記事の一部です。下の語群から最も適切なものを１つ選び、(　　　　) 内に記入しなさい。

"Looking 10 years ahead and solving problems is how new technologies are developed," Yoshino said. This strong resolve was the (　　　　) for his innovation.

Soon after Yoshino joined Asahi Kasei in 1972, he spent all his time conducting research (　　　　) at finding new uses for chemical compounds. He came up with various (　　　　), such as a film that would make glass harder to break and insulating materials that would not (　　　　) burn, but none led to a commercialized product.

A turning point came in the 10th year of Yoshino's steady research. He started (　　　　) whether polyacetylene, a polymer with high conductivity (　　　　) by Hideki Shirakawa, professor emeritus at the University of Tsukuba, who won the 2000 Nobel Prize in Chemistry, could be used as a material for batteries. This (　　　　) idea led to the development of a special carbon material that enabled batteries to be much (　　　　).

aimed	considering	discovered	easily
ideas	impetus	novel	smaller

Unit 9

●サウジ社会の変化はコーヒーハウスを覗けば分かる

イスラム教国サウジアラビアが変わりつつある。首都リヤドにあるコーヒーハウスの店内風景
Photo: The New York Times ／ Redux ／アフロ

Before you read

Kingdom of Saudi Arabia
サウジアラビア王国

面積　2,150,000km²（日本の約5.7倍）（世界12位）
人口　34,269,000人（世界41位）
首都　リアド
公用語　アラビア語
民族　サウジアラビア人　73%
　　　ヨーロッパ系　1%以下
　　　アラブ系　6%／アフリカ系　1%
　　　アジア系　20%
宗教　イスラム教スンニ派　85〜90%
　　　　　　　　シーア派　10〜15%
GDP　7,865億ドル（世界18位）
　　　1人当たりGDP　23,539ドル（世界40位）
通貨　サウジアラビア・リヤル
政体　君主制
識字率　94.8%

次の１〜５の語句の説明として最も近いものをａ〜ｅから１つ選び、（　　）内に記入しなさい。

1. on the front line   (   )   a. soaked
2. head-spinning   (   )   b. fast-changing and surprising
3. segregate   (   )   c. separate
4. skew   (   )   d. lean disproportionately toward
5. infused   (   )   e. at the leading edge

Summary

次の英文は記事の要約です。下の語群から最も適切な語を１つ選び、（　　）内に記入しなさい。

50

Saudi society is changing fast, with cafes (   ) this most clearly. Until recently, men and women had to be separated in (   ) places, but in many cafes both sexes are now (   ). In more (   ) cities like Jeddah young women can be seen chatting in cafes without head scarves. Some are (   ) working as baristas.

even	liberal	mixing	public	showing

　　サウジアラビアは、ベネズエラに次ぐ世界２位の石油埋蔵量・生産量・輸出量を誇るエネルギー大国である。輸出総額の約９割、財政収入の約８割を石油に依存している。さらに、OPEC 石油輸出国機構の指導国として国際石油市場に強い影響力を有している。
　　イスラム教最大の聖地メッカと第２のメディナの二大聖地を擁するイスラム世界の中心的存在で、主導的役割を果たしている。しかし、2014年以降原油価格低迷で財政赤字に陥り、18年には付加価値税を導入し、財源確保に努めて来た。
　　2016年12月、初めて女性の選挙権・被選挙権が認められ、女性20名が当選した。さらに社会・経済改革計画「ビジョン2030」を発表し、文化や娯楽活動、スポーツの振興、女性の社会進出促進、製造業や観光業の振興を掲げた。サウジ人労働力の積極的利用、石油部門以外の発展に力を注ぎ、人材育成・民営化・外資導入・市場開放など諸改革に努めている。
　　2017年６月にサルマン国王の３番目の妻との間の副皇太子ムハンマドを皇太子に昇格した。皇太子は脱石油依存の経済改革を主導し、2019年12月11日、国営石油会社サウジアラムコを証券取引所タダウルに株式を上場した。上場時の株式時価総額は約１兆8800億ドルとなり、世界最大の上場会社となった。

Reading

51

Saudi Society Is Changing.
Just Take a Look at These Coffeehouses.

> As the government relaxes restrictions on men and women working and socializing together, coffeehouses are on the front lines of change.

RIYADH, Saudi Arabia — For insight into these head-spinning times in Saudi Arabia, where the ultraconservative social and religious codes that micromanage daily life seem to spring a new leak every month — women driving! movie
5 theaters! Usher and Akon rapping to sold-out crowds! — it sometimes pays to read the Google Maps reviews of specialty coffee shops.

52

"I visited this place and was in a total shock!" Tarak Alhamood, a customer at Nabt Fenjan, a Riyadh coffee shop,
10 raged online recently. "You're violating the rules of this country. I hope this place gets closed permanently."

The issue was the decision that made Nabt Fenjan a daring outpost of the new Riyadh: Originally opened only for women, the coffee shop began allowing male and female customers to
15 mix in late 2018.

The move propelled the cafe ahead of the law in the kingdom, where most restaurants and coffee shops are divided, by law and custom, into all-male "singles" sections and "family" sections for women and mixed family groups.
20 Men enter through separate doors and pay in separate lines; women sometimes eat behind partitions to ensure privacy from male strangers.

53

In early December, however, the government announced that businesses would no longer be required to segregate
25 customers — the latest expansion of the social reforms initiated by the de facto Saudi ruler, Crown Prince Mohammed bin Salman.

Some women whose families might previously have

insight into ~：~への洞察

head-spinning：頭がくらくらする

codes：規範

spring a new leak：新たに漏れ出る

Usher and Akon：～アッシャーとエイコン《共に米国人歌手》

sold-out crowds：チケット売り切れのコンサート会場に集まった大勢の人

pays：良い、得になる

specialty coffee shops：コーヒー専門店

daring outpost：向こう見ずな前哨基地

move：行動、戦略

strangers：見知らぬ人

segregate ～：～を分離する

de facto：事実上の

Crown Prince：皇太子

allowed them to work only in the privacy of offices, if at
all, now hold barista jobs. Saudis can now mingle with the
opposite sex not only at home but also at movie theaters,
concerts and even wrestling matches. Young entrepreneurs
are opening places where Saudis can meet like-minded
people of both sexes, whether they are artists, filmmakers or
entrepreneurs.

54

The clientele in such coffee shops skews young, reflecting a
country where more than two-thirds of the population is under
30 and an unknown proportion is chronically bored. Bars are
barred, concerts and movies just starting to become widely
available. Evenings out, therefore, still tend to revolve around
food and (nonalcoholic) drink, the more Instagrammable, the
better.

Most coffee shops are still gender-segregated. But many
have other draws: imported Japanese brewing equipment,
Instagrammable tarts and — more intangible, but mandatory
nevertheless — good vibes.

55

Virtually none offer the golden, cardamom-infused Arabic
coffee, poured from a curvaceous pot into dainty cups and
served to guests with a hillock of dates, that traditionally
defined Saudi coffee culture.

Instead, at Draft, which still separates single men and
"families," there are quinoa salads and blond-wood tables
illuminated by industrial-style bulbs. And Medd Café in
Jeddah, the Red Sea city where social codes have long been
more relaxed than elsewhere, the organic, fair-trade beans are
roasted in-house.

On a recent Friday night at Medd Café, the outdoor patio
was crowded with young men and women. Many of the
women wore their hair uncovered and their abayas open over
jeans and sneakers, styling them more like long, fluid jackets
than the traditional all-covering gowns.

The New York Times, January 15, 2020

---

in the privacy of 〜：〜で
こっそりと

if at all：仮にあったとし
ても

barista：バリスタ《カフェ
でエスプレッソコーヒー
をつくる専門職人》

like-minded：同じ考えを持
った、同好の

clientele：常連客

skews young：若い人たち
に偏る

bored：退屈している

barred：禁じられている《イ
スラム教では飲酒は禁止》

revolve around 〜：〜を中
心に展開する

Instagrammable：インスタ
映えする

draws：魅力あるもの、人
を引き付けるもの

brewing equipment：エス
プレッソマシン、抽出機

intangible：触れることの
できない

vibes：雰囲気

cardamom-infused 〜：〜
カルダモン（香辛料）入
りの

dainty：小ぶりの

dates：ナツメヤシの実

quinoa：キノア《雑穀の一種》

blond-wood：ブロンド・ウ
ッド製の《blond wood；ブ
ロンド色の木材》

industrial-style bulbs：産
業用電球

fair-trade：フェアトレード
《農産物を買う際に、生産
者が適切な収入を得られ
るように適正価格を支払
う運動》

patio：中庭

abayas：アバヤ《アラビア
半島の女性の全身を覆う
伝統的衣装》

styling 〜：〜を着こなす

fluid：優雅な、流麗な

Exercises

次の１～３の英文を完成させ、４～５の英文の質問に答えるために、a～dの中から最も適切なものを１つ選びなさい。

1. The old rules when Nabt Fenjan first opened were that

    a. men and women customers had to sit separately.

    b. men had to enter through separate doors.

    c. women sometimes were required to eat behind partitions, out of view of the men.

    d. men were not allowed in the café.

2. Women are surprisingly allowed to

    a. stay home and not go into business.

    b. become baristas in coffee shops.

    c. drink alcohol.

    d. take care of their family.

3. Artists, filmmakers and entrepreneurs are described as

    a. concealing their creative activities from others.

    b. enjoying quinoa salads while conversing with other creative people.

    c. increasingly able to meet with individuals who have similar interests.

    d. unable to benefit from the changes in Saudi Arabia.

4. What percentage of the population in Saudi Arabia are under 30 years old?

    a. Under 6%.

    b. Around 30%.

    c. About 33%.

    d. Over 66%.

5. What do traditional coffee shop offer customers?

    a. Organic fair-trade fresh roasted beans.

    b. Quinoa salads.

    c. Arabic coffee and dates.

    d. Cappuccino coffee.

True or False

本文の内容に合致するものに T（True）、合致しないものに F（False）をつけなさい。

(　) **1.** Women are now allowed to drive a car.

(　) **2.** Usher and Akon were not allowed to perform in Saudi Arabia.

(　) **3.** Most coffee shops are still gender-segregated.

(　) **4.** Crown Prince Mohammad bin Salman is largely responsible for the social reform in Saudi Arabia.

(　) **5.** Tables in coffee shops are not allowed to have industrial-style bulbs.

Vocabulary

次の英文は、The New York Times に掲載された *Aramco Sets I.P.O. Target: $25.6 Billion*『アラムコ、新規公開株 I.P.O ２兆56億ドル上場』の記事の一部です。下の語群から最も適切なものを１つ選び、(　) 内に記入しなさい。

Saudi Arabia's giant state-(　) oil company, Saudi Aramco, on Thursday set the price of its initial public offering at a level that would raise $25.6 billion, a sum that is expected to make it the world's (　) I.P.O.

The I.P.O. will establish Aramco as one of the world's most (　) companies, but the $1.7 trillion figure falls (　) of the Saudi royal family's hopes of an offering that valued the company at close to $2 trillion.

Global investors proved to be (　) over the earlier valuations offered by the Saudi government. While its filings showed Aramco to be immensely profitable – it posted a profit of $68 billion for the first nine months of the year – its earnings have declined, and risks like global (　) and geopolitical instability cast a pall over its prospects.

The I.P.O. process has been agonizingly slow since Crown Prince Mohammed bin Salman, Saudi Arabia's de facto ruler, first raised the idea of making the crown (　) of the Saudi economy a public company more than two years ago.

After big early promises, the Saudis have taken a more cautious approach, restricting the listing initially to Saudi Arabia in order to (　) the more rigorous disclosures that would be required in New York or London.

avoid	biggest	jewel	owned
short	skittish	valuable	warming

Unit 10

●移民流入は壁では阻止できない

米国カリフォルニア州シリコンバレーのサニーベールにあるインド服飾専門店

Photo: The New York Times ／ Redux ／アフロ

Before you read

United States of America
アメリカ合衆国

面積　9,628,000km²（日本の約25.5倍）（世界３位）
人口　327,750,000人（世界３位）
首都　ワシントンDC
最大都市　ニューヨーク
公用語　なし、事実上は英語
識字率　93.5%
人種　白人　72.4%／ヒスパニック　18.5%
　　　黒人　12.7%／アジア系　4.8%
　　　ネイティブアメリカン　0.9%
宗教　キリスト教・カトリック　20%
　　　キリスト教・プロテスタント　57%
　　　ユダヤ教　1.3%
　　　イスラム教　0.9%
　　　無宗教　20.8%
GDP　20兆5802億ドル（世界１位）
　　　１人当たりGDP　62,869ドル（世界９位）
通貨　USドル
政体　大統領制・連邦制

次の１〜５の語の説明として最も近いものをａ〜ｅから１つ選び、（　）内に記入しなさい。

1. deter　　　　　　（　）　　a. walk through water
2. undocumented　　（　）　　b. heavily
3. round-around　　 （　）　　c. dissuade
4. wade　　　　　　（　）　　d. long and complicated route
5. overwhelmingly　（　）　　e. without legal papers or permission

Summary

　次の英文は記事の要約です。下の語群から最も適切な語を１つ選び、（　）内に記入しなさい。

Since Trump became president, discussion about (　　　　　) immigration has focused on the (　　　　　) border with Mexico. But almost half America's undocumented residents entered by air and (　　　　　) immigration checks. They only became illegal when they (　　　　) to return on time. Officials have been (　　　　　) to keep track of all of the thousands who simply decide to stay.

　　completed　　failed　　illegal　　land　　unable

　アメリカが迎い入れた移民の数は、世界のどの国よりも多く、5,000万人を超えている。Trump 政権になっても年間70万人近い移民を受け入れている。1990年のアメリカの人口のうち2,000万人は、外国生まれだった。ニューヨーク湾内のエリス島にある自由の女神像の台座にエマ・ラザルスの詩の一節「疲れし者、貧しき者を我に与えよ。自由の空気を吸わんと熱望する人たちよ…、身を寄せ合う哀れな人たちよ。住む家なく、嵐にもまれし者を我に送りたまえ。我は、黄金の扉にて灯を掲げん」が刻まれている。アメリカは、ヨーロッパ諸国からやって来た移民たちに自由と希望を与えた黄金の扉だった。

　しかし、1619年から1808年までの間、強制的に奴隷として連れて来られた50万人のアフリカ人もいる。今日アフリカ系アメリカ人は、総人口の12.7%を占めている。さらに、スペイン語圏の出身者ヒスパニック系の移民も1970年代から急増し、今日約2,700万人もいる。５割はメキシコ系である。また、今日、アジア系アメリカ人が約1,000万人いるが、最も成功度の高い移民グループだ。今日約500万人の不法滞在者がいて、年間27万5,000人の割合で増え、社会福祉制度に大きな負担となっている。1986年に移民法が改正され、90万人が合法的に滞在する資格を得た。

Reading

57

An Immigrant Influx That a Wall Won't Deter

Immigrant Influx：移民の流入

Deter ～：～を阻止する

| Millions Who Legally Enter the United States As Students or Tourists Never Go Back |

SUNNYVALE, Calif.—Eddie Oh, an industrial engineer, lost his job during the financial crisis that gripped South Korea in 1998. With no prospects, he scrounged together his savings to pay his family's airfare to California. They were
5 going on vacation, he told the United States embassy, which issued six-month visitor visas for the family.

financial crisis：金融危機

With no prospects：見込みはない

They ～ vacation：《told の直接目的語》

visitor visas：観光ビザ

58

The Ohs headed to Sunnyvale, a middle-class community in California's Silicon Valley where a relative already had rented a small apartment. The Ohs moved in, nine people
10 crammed into two rooms. Mr. Oh got to work painting houses. His wife found a job as a waitress. And their children, Eli, 11, and Sue, 9, started school.

"We were constantly in debt. We struggled to pay the rent," said Eli Oh, who grew up to be a critical-care response
15 nurse at Stanford University. "Nobody ever thought we were illegally here, because we didn't fit the stereotype."

in debt：借金している

critical-care response nurse：救命救急対応看護師

stereotype：固定観念、イメージ

59

They are hardly alone. Though President Trump has staked much of his presidency on halting the movement of undocumented immigrants across the southern border, the Oh
20 family's round-around route to residence in the United States is part of one of America's least widely known immigration stories.

undocumented：ビザや ID のない

least ～：ほとんど～でない

Some 350,000 travelers arrive by air in the United States each day. From Asia, South America and Africa, they come
25 mostly with visas allowing them to tour, study, do business or attend a conference for an authorized period of time.

authorized：認定された

Nearly half of the estimated 11 million undocumented immigrants now in the country did not trek through the desert or wade across the Rio Grande to enter the country; they flew
30 in with a visa, passed inspection at the airport—and stayed.

inspection：審査

Many undocumented Asians—including a large number from India—have settled like the Ohs in and around Sunnyvale, about 50 miles southeast of San Francisco, according to the Center for Migration Studies analysis.

35   Apple, LinkedIn and other tech titans in the area employ many whom the companies have sponsored for legal work visas or permanent residency in the United States.

Some of them stay on as independent programming contractors after their visas have expired or after leaving a
40 company that sponsored them for a visa.

But developing policies to curb overstays requires accurate data, experts say, and Homeland Security officials still lack a reliable system to track them.

Most travelers are photographed and fingerprinted at
45 American consulates abroad when they receive a visa and then again on arrival in the United States. But Customs and Border Protection still depends overwhelmingly on biographical information from the manifests of departing travelers, provided by airlines, to tally who did not leave in
50 time, or at all.

Immigration and Customs Enforcement, which enforces immigration rules in the interior of the country, said that it puts a priority on identifying those who pose potential national security or public-safety threats. In fiscal 2018, its Homeland
55 Security Investigations unit made 1,808 arrests in connection with visa-violation leads.

The New York Times, December 2, 2019

settled in 〜：〜に住み着く

Center for Migration
  Studies：移民研究センタ
  ー《ニューヨークを本拠
  とするシンクタンク》

LinkedIn：リンクトイン
  《世界最大級のビジネス型
  SNS; 親会社はマイクロソ
  フト》

permanent residency：永住
  権

contractors：請負（受託）
  業者

expired：有効期限が切れた

curb overstays：ビザが切れ
  た不法滞在者を抑制する

Homeland Security：国土安
  全保障省《各国の内務省
  に相当》

consulates：領事館

Customs and Border
  Protection：税関・国境
  取締局《国土安全保障省
  の一部門》

biographical
  information：略歴

manifests：乗客名簿

tally 〜：〜を記録する

Immigration and Customs
  Enforcement：移民・関
  税執行局《国土安全保障
  省の一部門》

immigration rules：入国管
  理法令

identifying 〜：〜を割り
  出す
pose potential threats：脅
  威をもたらしかねない

fiscal：会計年度

Homeland Security
  Investigations unit：米国
  の安全に関する捜査部

visa-violation leads：不正
  ビザの「おとり捜査」

Exercises

Multiple Choice

次の１の英文の質問に答え、２〜５の英文を完成させるために、ａ〜ｄの中から最も適切なものを１つ選びなさい。

1. At the time of writing, about how many people flew into the U.S. each day?

    a. 3,500.
    b. 50,000.
    c. 300,000.
    d. 350,000.

2. The Oh family entered the U.S.

    a. illegally.
    b. with legal visas.
    c. fitting the popular stereotype of immigrants.
    d. intending to return to South Korea.

3. Half of the immigrants in the U.S.

    a. trekked through the desert to get into the country.
    b. waded across the Rio Grande from Mexico.
    c. flew in legally as tourists and overstayed their visas.
    d. climbed the border fence in order to get in.

4. Sunnyvale, California is known for

    a. high tech companies like Apple.
    b. offering many job opportunities.
    c. its peaceful middle-class community.
    d. all of the above features.

5. The author feels that President Trump's beloved wall

    a. will mostly solve the problem of immigration "overstays."
    b. will be far too expensive to be completed.
    c. has managed to reduce illegal immigration to a large degree.
    d. is irrelevant to the way many illegal immigrants enter the U.S.

本文の内容に合致するものに T（True）、合致しないものに F（False）をつけなさい。

(　　) **1.** Eli Oh became a critical care nurse at Stanford.

(　　) **2.** There are currently 6 million undocumented immigrants in the U.S.

(　　) **3.** The Ohs' first jobs helped them get started and established in their new country.

(　　) **4.** Apple, LinkedIn and other tech companies sometimes sponsor employees for permanent residency in the U.S.

(　　) **5.** The U.S. Embassy never issues 6-month visas.

Vocabulary

次の英文は、Pew Research Center の Fact Tank News in the Numbers: *Key findings about U.S. immigrants*『アメリカの移民に関する主な調査結果』の一部です。下の語群から最も適切なものを１つ選び、（　　）内に記入しなさい。

The United States has (　　　　　　) immigrants than any other country in the world. Today, more than 40 million people living in the U.S. were born in (　　　　　　) country, accounting for about one-fifth of the world's (　　　　　) in 2017. The population of immigrants is also very (　　　　　), with just about every country in the world represented among U.S. immigrants.

Most immigrants (77%) are in the country (　　　　　), while almost a quarter are unauthorized. In 2017, 45% were naturalized U.S. citizens. Some 27% of immigrants were permanent residents and 5% were (　　　　　) residents in 2017.

The decline in the unauthorized immigrant population is due largely to a (　　　　　) in the number from Mexico. Meanwhile, there was a rise in the number from Central America and Asia.

Generally, most immigrants eligible for naturalization apply to become citizens. However, Mexican lawful immigrants have the lowest naturalization rate overall. (　　　　　) and personal barriers, lack of interest and financial barriers are the top reasons for choosing not to naturalize cited by Mexican-born green card holders.

another	diverse	fall	language
legally	migrants	more	temporary

Unit 11

- 「桜戦士」、チームの結束を称賛
- 日本のファンは歴史的成果を褒めちぎる

ラグビー・ワールドカップ1次リーグでのスコットランドとの最終戦で勝利し喜ぶ「桜戦士」
Photo: Kyodo News

Before you read

次の a 〜 h のラグビーに該当するものを①〜⑧の中から選びなさい。

a. forward （　） ① putting the ball into play at the start of the first or second half

b. half-time （　） ② taking hold of a player and making them fall

c. line-out （　） ③ the interval between the two halves of the game

d. kickoff （　） ④ a free kick

e. penalty kick （　） ⑤ five points won by grounding the ball

f. scrum(mage) （　） ⑥ the players pushing together with their heads down

g. tackle （　） ⑦ restarting play by throwing the ball in from the sideline

h. try （　） ⑧ player who competes for the ball in a scrum

次の1〜5の語句の説明として最も近いものをa〜eから1つ選び、（　）内に記入しなさい。

1. make a run　　（　　）　　　　a. say or do something similar
2. echo　　　　　（　　）　　　　b. able to
3. capable of　　（　　）　　　　c. not quite reaching a goal
4. short of　　　（　　）　　　　d. act as organizer and inviter
5. host　　　　　（　　）　　　　e. progress through several rounds

次の英文は記事の要約です。下の語群から最も適切な語を1つ選び、（　　）内に記入しなさい。

Japan's squad (　　　　　　) the last eight at the Rugby World Cup on home territory.　The Brave Blossoms (　　　　　) their previous performances.　On the way they (　　　　　) Ireland and Scotland, two nations with long rugby traditions.　Coach Jamie Joseph (　　　　　) the achievement to the players' hard work, while team member Michael Leitch also (　　　　　) the importance of unity.

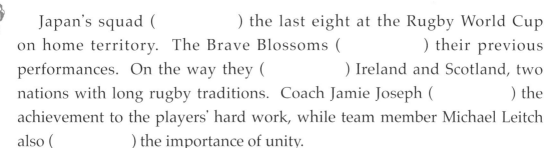

attributed　　defeated　　exceeded　　made　　stressed

　　1823年イングランドのパブリックスクール・ラグビー校でフットボールの試合中に、William Web Ellis がボールを抱えたまま相手のゴール目指して走り出した。1840年にはボールを持って走る「running in」が確立、普及し出した。その当時、現代のサッカーは生まれておらず、Ellis が手でボールを扱ったことではなく、ボールを持って走った行為が、フットボールではルール違反だった。現在のラグビーは、13人制の rugby league と15人制の rugby union がある。日本のラグビーは通常 rugby union である。

　　2019年10月にラグビーワールドカップ日本大会が行われた。日本チーム「桜戦士」は開幕戦でロシアに快勝し、ワールドカップ優勝候補のアイルランドから歴史的金星を挙げた。続くサモア戦で4トライを奪って勝利し、強豪スコットランド戦では相手の猛攻に耐えてグループリーグ4連勝で1位通過し、初めて8強入りを果たし、日本中に熱狂をもたらした。準々決勝で南アフリカに敗れたものの、国籍や出身地を超えてチーム一丸となって戦う姿に日本中が熱狂し、「にわかファン」という造語も登場した。チームのスローガン「One Team ワンチーム」が2019年度の新語・流行語大賞に選ばれた。さらに6,464億円の経済波及効果をもたらした。

Reading

63

Brave Blossoms praise team unity

Japan coach Jamie Joseph said Monday the team's impressive work ethic played a major role in the hosts making a run to the Rugby World Cup's last eight for the first time.

Speaking a day after the Brave Blossoms were knocked
5 out of the tournament via a 26-3 defeat to South Africa, Joseph said "the team had worked incredibly hard for the last three years."

He also paid tribute to the players who did not make the World Cup squad, saying they "had contributed just as much."

64

10 Joseph's future with the national team remains in doubt due to difficulties that have arisen regarding his proposed contract extension, according to sources.

But no matter what happens next, he wanted to make sure he thanked the nation for their support and the players for
15 their belief in what he was trying to achieve.

Michael Leitch echoed his coach, saying the team's unity played a big role in their ability to go through the pool stages unbeaten, defeating two Tier One sides along the way.

"I'm proud to be the captain of this team," he said. "I'm
20 happy we made the best eight. The reason we got this far is because Jamie united us and made us one team."

65

Four years ago, the Japan Rugby Football Union failed to ride the momentum of Japan's success in England and the players spoke of their hope that this time around things would
25 be different.

"When we came back from New Zealand after the 2011 tournament, there were only two or three reporters, so it's unbelievable to see so many of you here today," hooker Shota Horie said of the news conference, which was broadcast live
30 on TV.

66

"It's our mission to work toward the next World Cup and keep up the popularity of rugby. What matters is how much

---

Brave Blossoms：「桜戦士」、ラグビー日本代表《胸のエンブレムが桜》

work ethic：労働意欲

hosts making a run to ～：開催国の日本代表が～まで一気に駆け上がったこと

last eight：ベスト8

via ～：～によって

defeat to ～：～に敗北

paid tribute to ～：～を称賛した

make the World Cup squad：ワールドカップに出場するチームに参加する

contract extension：契約延長

sources：消息筋

no matter what happens：何が起きようが

echoed ～：～に同調した

pool stages：予選リーグ

Tier One sides：一流チーム

Japan Rugby Football Union：日本ラグビー・フットボール協会《公益財団法人；日本におけるラグビーの高校・大学・ジャパンラグビートップリーグを総括する国内競技連盟》

momentum：勢い

success：活躍

this time around：今度は

hooker：フッカー《フォワード最前列中央のプレーヤー；スクラムの際、ボールを味方の方へかき出す》

Shota Horie：堀江翔太

What matters：大事なのは

stronger and better we can get from here on," Horie said.

Flyhalf Yu Tamura, who broke a rib during the defeat to
35 South Africa, said he had "realized through this tournament that we're capable of doing our very best and becoming the national team that everyone admires and wants to join."

Japanese fans laud historic effort

Japan fell a win short of making the final four at the Rugby
40 World Cup, but both those involved in the game and others watching from the outside said Sunday they are proud of what the team achieved.

"Watching them beat Ireland, then Scotland (in the pool stages), it was more than I thought was possible. I want
45 Japan to keep improving and win the World Cup one day," Yokohama resident Musashi Oka said after watching Japan lose its quarterfinal 26-3 to South Africa from a fan zone outside Oita Station.

The 27-year-old, among hundreds of Japanese and foreign
50 fans in Oita, said meeting rugby fans from around the world has been a highlight of the World Cup so far. "It's been so much fun, I hope we can host it again," he said.

The Japan Times based on Kyodo, October 22, 2019

Flyhalf：フライハーフ、スタンドオフ《チームの司令塔で背番号10；ハーフ団の一員でよくボールを蹴り上げる》
Yu Tamura：田村優
realized 〜：〜を実感した

laud 〜：〜を褒めちぎる
effort：成果

fell a win short of making the final four：勝ってベスト4進出に届かなかった
involved in 〜：〜に関わった

more than I thought was possible：期待していた以上

quarterfinal：準々決勝
fan zone：ファンゾーン会場《大型スクリーンでの観戦が出来る広場》

Exercises

次の1〜5の英文を完成させるために、a〜dの中から最も適切なものを1つ選びなさい。

1. The Japan coach of the rugby team
   a. praised the team's work ethic.
   b. complained about the players losing the game against South Africa.
   c. told the team he will not return as their coach in the future.
   d. forgot to thank the nation for their support.

2. The captain of the Brave Blossoms was
   a. Yu Tamura.
   b. Shota Horie.
   c. Michael Leitch.
   d. Jamie Joseph.

3. At the news conference, Horie
   a. expressed his optimism about the next World Cup.
   b. contrasted the reception in 2019 with the atmosphere eight years before.
   c. hoped that rugby would maintain its popularity in Japan.
   d. made all of the above comments.

4. The World Cup game this past year was held in
   a. South Africa.
   b. Japan.
   c. England.
   d. Scotland.

5. For one fan from Yokohama a highlight of the World Cup was
   a. watching the game from Oita station.
   b. dreaming of the day when Japan will win the competition.
   c. meeting and interacting with rugby-lovers from Japan and around the world.
   d. passing, and running with the ball alongside his heroes.

本文の内容に合致するものに T（True）、合致しないものに F（False）をつけなさい。

(   ) **1.** Though Japan did not win, they contributed to an historic event.

(   ) **2.** The captain of the team had few nice words to say about his coach.

(   ) **3.** One player, Yu Tamura, broke a rib in a game with South Africa.

(   ) **4.** Only 2 or 3 reporters came to the airport to see the team arrive after the 2019 tournament.

(   ) **5.** The coach is currently in serious negotiations about his contract for next year.

Vocabulary

1～12 の「rugby ground」の呼称に該当するものをイラスト a ～ l の中から 1 つ選び、（   ）内に記入しなさい。

1. crossbar (   )
2. dead ball line (   )
3. five yards line (   )
4. goal line (   )
5. goal post (   )
6. halfway line (   )
7. hooker (   )
8. referee (   )
9. scrum half (   )
10. ten yards line (   )
11. touchline (   )
12. twenty-five yards line (   )

● ソマリアの若者たち、政府機能不全の地域に足を踏み入れる

内戦が続くソマリアの首都モガディシュで82名が死亡し、約150名が負傷した爆弾テロ現場

Photo: The New York Times ／ Redux ／アフロ

Before you read

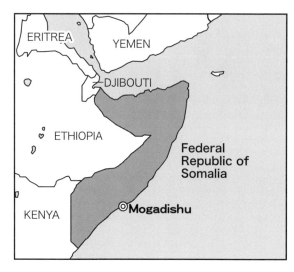

Federal Republic of Somalia
ソマリア連邦共和国

面積　638,000km²（日本の約1.8倍）（世界42位）
首都　モガディシュ
公用語　ソマリ語・アラビア語
人口　15,443,000人（世界73位）
民族　ソマリ族　85%
宗教　イスラム教
識字率　37.8%
GDP　4,721,000,000ドル（世界155位）
　　　　1人当たり GDP　1,815ドル（世界148位）
通貨　ソマリア・シリング
政体　連邦共和制

Words and Phrases

次の1～5の語の説明として最も近いものをa～eから1つ選び、（　）内に記入しなさい。

1. anemic   （　）   a. lacking iron in the blood
2. spring   （　）   b. weighed down by demands
3. overwhelmed （　）   c. torment
4. bedevil   （　）   d. increase
5. amplify   （　）   e. respond quickly and actively

Summary

次の英文は記事の要約です。下の語群から最も適切な語を1つ選び、（　）内に記入しなさい。

Somalia's government sometimes seems unable to (　　　　) with the diseases, floods, terrorism and other problems it faces. Increasingly, however, its younger (　　　　) are responding to crises directly. They (　　　　) in medical facilities, organize support for (　　　　) and even build roads. Some have returned from overseas (　　　　) to rebuild their country.

> cope   determined   generation   victims   volunteer

1886年に英国が北部を英領ソマリランドとして領有し、1908年までにイタリアが南部を領土とした。1960年7月1日英領北部とイタリア領南部が統合、独立し、ソマリア共和国が発足した。1969年のクーデターによりバレ政権が実権を握り、ソマリ社会主義革命党の一党独裁体制となった。1988年に内戦勃発、91年にバレ政権が崩壊した。

崩壊以来2007年まで、ソマリアは全土を実効的に支配する中央政府が存在しない状態が続いた。劣悪な治安の下、大量の難民及び国内避難民が発生し、また干ばつの深刻化等により、食糧不足が悪化する等、重大な人道危機が生じた。

2012年9月にハッサン・モハムドが大統領に選出され、21年振りに統一政府が樹立された。2017年には、モハメド・ファルマージョが新大統領に選出された。アラブ・アフリカ諸国との友好関係の維持を外交の基盤とし、国造りと国際社会の支援を要請している。

ソマリア沖・アデン湾の海賊発生件数は、近年低い水準で推移している。一方、海賊を生み出す根本原因の1つであるソマリア国内の貧困や若者の就職難等は未だ解決しておらず、海賊による脅威は引き続き存在している。経済も壊滅状態で、最貧国の1つである。

Reading

69

Young Somalis Step in Where Government Fails

MOGADISHU, Somalia — She had just finished battling the floods, and then the bomb went off.

For a month of 10-hour days, Dr. Amina Abdulkadir Isack, 27, tended to anemic mothers, children with malaria
5 and pregnant women as a volunteer in central Somalia, where record floods had left thousands of people in dire need of help the government could scarcely provide.

70

But only days after she came home, on a hot Mogadishu morning in late December, terrorists detonated an explosives-
10 laden truck in a busy intersection, killing 82 people and injuring nearly 150, including university students studying to become health specialists and doctors like her.

Dr. Isack sprang right back into action, helping a youth-led crisis response team of volunteers who tracked the victims,
15 called their families, collected donations and performed many services the government was too overwhelmed to manage on its own.

"The youth are the ones who build nations," Dr. Isack said. "We have to rely on ourselves."

71
20 Much like the floods before it, the attack in Mogadishu, the deadliest in Somalia in more than two years, underscored the feeble emergency response in a nation that is no stranger to natural and man-made disasters. The Somali government struggles to provide basic public services like health care and
25 education, let alone a comprehensive response to emergencies.

Yet in the face of the country's mounting challenges — from a changing climate to the indiscriminate violence of terrorism — young Somalis are increasingly getting organized and bootstrapping their way out of crises, rather than waiting
30 on help from their government or its foreign backers.

72
Government officials say they do respond to the country's emergencies, including establishing a national committee

went off：爆発した

For a month of 10-hour days：1日10時間を一か月間

tended to ～：～の世話をした

anemic：貧血症の

busy intersection：人通りの多い交差点

sprang back into action：勢いよく仕事を再開した

crisis response team of ～：～から成る危機対応チーム

tacked ～：～の身元を確認した

donations：寄付

on its own：自力では

underscored ～：～を明確に示した

no stranger to ～：～を全く知らないわけではない

let alone ～：～は言うまでもなく

indiscriminate：無差別な

organized：組織化された

bootstrapping their way out of ～：自力で～からの脱出を試みる

to aid the victims of the Dec. 28 attack. Turkey and Qatar airlifted dozens of the badly injured. But many youth activists in Somalia say that the response from the authorities is often tardy or inadequate, making it all the more essential for citizens like themselves to jump in and help fill the gaps.

Somalia has experienced one degree or another of chaos for almost three decades, bedeviled first by clan infighting and then by violent extremism. But through it all, Somalis have found ways to not only establish thriving businesses, but also take on core state services like building roads and providing health care and education.

73

This independent spirit was amplified after militants with the Shabab, a terrorist group affiliated with Al Qaeda, surrendered control of Mogadishu in 2011, effectively leaving the capital in the hands of an internationally-backed but weak government that has often been unable to secure the capital, much less the country.

Since then, young Somalis, including members of the diaspora who have returned home, have taken a leading role in the stabilization and rebuilding process. They have worked on rehabilitating child soldiers, reviving domestic tourism, responding to humanitarian crises, organizing book fairs and even selling Somali camels to customers using bitcoin.

The New York Times, February 16, 2020

tardy or inadequate：遅いか不充分な

all the more：増々

one degree or another of ～：程度の差がある～

bedeviled：苦しめられる

clan infighting：クラン（氏族・部族）間の内紛

take on ～：～に取り組む

core state services：国家による中核となるサービス

Shabab：アル・シャバブ《ソマリア南部を中心に活動するイスラム勢力》

Al Qaeda：アル・カイダ、国際イスラム戦線《アラビア語で「墓地」の意；国際的なテロのネットワーク》

surrendered control of ～：～の支配権を放棄した

leaving ～ in the hands of …：～を…の手に委ねる

much less ～：まして～ではない

diaspora who have returned home：国から離散したが帰国した人たち

stabilization：安定化

worked on ～：～に取り組んできた

rehabilitating ～：～の更生

bitcoin：ビットコイン《インターネット上の仮想通貨の一種》

Exercises

Multiple Choice

次の１〜２の英文の質問に答え、３〜５の英文を完成させるために、ａ〜ｄの中から最も
適切なものを１つ選びなさい。

1. Which group is credited in this article with keeping Somalia moving?

    a. Young Somalians.

    b. The government officials.

    c. The militants with Shabab.

    d. Turkish and Qatari aid-givers.

2. How many people were killed or injured in the bomb attack?

    a. 82 killed and 150 injured

    b. 150 killed and 82 injured.

    c. 230 killed and 15 injured.

    d. 380 killed.

3. The government has argued that it

    a. was tardy in dealing with natural disasters.

    b. depends entirely on youthful volunteers.

    c. cannot build roads without receiving foreign aid.

    d. responded to the bomb attack.

4. At only 27, Dr. Isack found herself having to

    a. surrender control of Mogadishu.

    b. defuse explosives loaded onto a truck in a busy intersection.

    c. enter politics because of the lack of government leadership.

    d. handle a major flood and organize volunteers to help bomb victims.

5. Somalia has had the kind of problems mentioned in this article for

    a. three years.

    b. thirteen decades.

    c. thirty years.

    d. a third of its history.

本文の内容に合致するものにT（True）、合致しないものにF（False）をつけなさい。

(　) **1.** The government's response to emergencies is generally adequate.

(　) **2.** Somalia has done better since Al Qaeda surrendered control over Mogadishu, allowing the spirit of young Somalians to shine.

(　) **3.** Two of the challenges of Somalia are a changing climate and terrorist attacks.

(　) **4.** It is not difficult for the country to acquire capital.

(　) **5.** Malaria still exists in Mogadishu.

Vocabulary

次の１〜８は、アフリカ中・東部の国々に関する英文です。 下記の国名から１つ選び（ 　 ）内に、ａ〜ｈを地図から選び、[　]内に記入しなさい。

1. (　　) has borders with Djibouti, Ethiopia, and Kenya and its capital is Mogadishu.　　　　　　　　　　[　]

2. (　　) is a country in eastern Africa and its capital is Addis Ababa.　　　　　　　　　　　　　　　　　[　]

3. (　　) 's capital is Nairobi and its main languages are English and Swahili.　　　　　　　　　　　　　[　]

4. (　　) is a small country and has a border with Somalia and Ethiopia.　　　　　　　　　　　　　　　[　]

5. (　　) is a united republic in the east with an Indian Ocean coast.　　　　　　　　　　　　　　　　[　]

6. (　　) 's people are called Rwandan.　　　　　　　[　]

7. (　　) is a country in the eastern central region and its capital is Kampala.　　　　　　　　　　　　[　]

8. (　　) has borders with Congo, Rwanda, and Tanzania.　[　]

Burundi	Djibouti
Ethiopia	Kenya
Rwanda	Somalia
Tanzania	Uganda

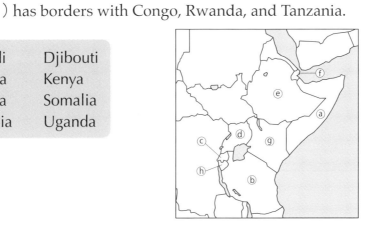

13

●新国籍法への反対運動が荒れ狂うが、インドは ヒンドゥ教国となるのか

インドでイスラム教徒を除外する新国籍法を巡り、抗議するデモ参加者たち

Photo: ロイター／アフロ

Before you read

Republic of India　インド

面積　3,287,590km²（日本の8.7倍）（世界７位）
人口　1,310,000,000人（世界２位）
首都　ニューデリー　／ デリー連邦直轄地
最大都市　ムンバイ
公用語　英語、ヒンドゥ語
民族　インド・アーリア族　72%
　　　ドラヴィダ族　25%
　　　モンゴロイド族　3%
宗教　ヒンドゥ教　79.8%
　　　イスラム教　14.2%
　　　キリスト教　2.3%　／ シーク教　1.7%
　　　仏教　0.7%　／ ジャイナ教　0.4%
GDP　２兆7,187億ドル（世界７位）
　　　１人当たりGDP　2,038ドル（世界144位）
通貨　インド・ルビー
識字率　75.6%
政体　共和制

次の1～5の語句の説明として最も近いものをa～eから1つ選び、(　　)内に記入しなさい。

1. round up	(　　)		**a.**	centered on religion
2. overt	(　　)		**b.**	cut or disconnect
3. shut down	(　　)		**c.**	open and obvious
4. wrench	(　　)		**d.**	arrest many people
5. theocratic	(　　)		**e.**	pull forcefully

Summary

次の英文は記事の要約です。下の語群から最も適切な語を1つ選び、(　　)内に記入しなさい。

74

The Modi government says its new citizenship law will (　　　　　　) immigrants. However, the measure (　　　　　　) Muslims. The government argues that it is (　　　　　　) who need support as they are often escaping Muslim-majority countries. But India's large Muslim (　　　　　　) claims this is part of a campaign to (　　　　　　) against them and strengthen the Hindu majority.

discriminate　　　excludes　　　help　　　minority　　　non-Muslims

　　2019年12月に、インドの議会で改正国籍法が可決され、成立した。従来の国籍法に、イスラム教徒ではないバングラディシュとパキスタンとアフガニスタンから2014年末までにインドに逃れてきた不法移民に対して国籍を与えるとする条項が加わった。イスラム教徒は対象外で、ヒンドゥ教、仏教、キリスト教、ジャイナ教などの6宗教の信者で、迫害を受けた宗教的少数者を想定している。

　　3か国であるバングラディシュには88.4％、パキスタンは97％、アフガニスタン99％のイスラム教徒がいて、大多数を占めている。しかし、この改正国籍法では、イスラム教徒は対象外になり、最終的にイスラム教徒だけが不法滞在者となってしまう。これは、イスラム教の排除につながり、宗教対立が起きている。首都ニューデリーでは、52名の死者が出て、惨事となった。この改正国籍法への賛成派と反対派による大規模な衝突も起きているが、モディ首相は強気の姿勢を崩していない。

　　モディ首相率いる与党インド人民党は、ヒンドゥ教に基づく国家運営を目指すヒンドゥ教至上主義を掲げている。しかし、インドもコロナウイルス感染拡大防止のため、2020年4月から Lockdown が続いている。

Reading

As Protests Rage on Citizenship Bill, Is India Becoming a Hindu Nation?

NEW DELHI — Prime Minister Narendra Modi's government has rounded up thousands of Muslims in Kashmir, revoked the area's autonomy and enforced a citizenship test in northeastern India that left nearly two million people
5 potentially stateless, many of them Muslim.

But it was Mr. Modi's gamble to pass a sweeping new citizenship law that favors every South Asian faith other than Islam that has set off days of widespread protests.

The law, which easily passed both houses of Parliament
10 last week, is the most overt sign, opponents say, that Mr. Modi intends to turn India into a Hindu-centric state that would leave the country's 200 million Muslims at a calculated disadvantage.

Indian Muslims, who have watched anxiously as Mr.
15 Modi's government has pursued a Hindu nationalist program, have finally erupted in anger. Over the past few days, protests have broken in cities across the country.

Mr. Modi's government has responded by calling out troops, shutting down the internet and imposing curfews, just
20 as it did when it clamped down on Kashmir. In New Delhi, police officers beat unarmed students with wooden poles, dragging them away and sending scores to the hospital. In Assam, they shot and killed several young men.

India's Muslims had stayed relatively quiet during the
25 other recent setbacks, keenly aware of the electoral logic that has pushed them to the margins. India is about 80 percent Hindu, and 14 percent Muslim, and Mr. Modi and his party won a crushing election victory in May and handily control the Parliament.

30 But Indian Muslims are feeling increasingly desperate, and so are progressives, many Indians of other faiths, and

Citizenship Bill：国籍法《改正法でインドに住む不法移民にインド国籍を与えるのが目的》

rounded up ～：～を逮捕した

revoked ～：～を取り消した、無効にした

autonomy：自治権

favors ～：～をえこひいきする

other than ～：～以外の

both houses：上下両院

opponents：反対派

calculated disadvantage：事前に目論まれた不利益

nationalist：民族主義的

erupted in anger：怒りを爆発させた

broken：突然発生した

curfews：（夜間）外出禁止令

clamped down on ～：～を弾圧した

setbacks：敗北、後退

keenly aware of ～：～を痛感させられる

his party：インド人民党

progressives：進歩主義者

those who see a secular government as fundamental to India's identity and its future.

78

35　The world is now weighing in, too. United Nations officials, American representatives, international advocacy groups and religious organizations have issued scathing statements saying that the citizenship law is blatantly discriminatory. Some are even calling for sanctions.

40　Critics are deeply worried that Mr. Modi is trying to wrench India away from its secular, democratic roots and turn this nation of 1.3 billion people into a religious state, a homeland for Hindus.

　　"They want a theocratic state," said B.N. Srikrishna, a former judge on India's Supreme Court. "This is pushing the
45　country to the brink, to the brink of chaos."

79

　　Mr. Modi is no stranger to communal violence. The worst bloodshed that India has seen in recent years exploded on his watch, in 2002, in Gujarat, when he was the top official in the state and clashes between Hindus and Muslims killed more
50　than 1,000 people — most of them Muslims.

　　The new citizenship legislation, called the Citizenship Amendment Act, expedites Indian citizenship for migrants from some of India's neighboring countries if they are Hindu, Christian, Buddhist, Sikh, Parsee or Jain. Only one major
55　religion in South Asia was left off: Islam.

　　Indian officials have denied any anti-Muslim bias and said the measure was intended purely to help persecuted minorities migrating from India's predominantly Muslim neighbors — Pakistan, Afghanistan and Bangladesh.

The New York Times, December 16, 2019

---

secular government：非宗教政権

weighing in：介入する

representatives：国会議員
advocacy groups：権利擁護団体

discriminatory：差別的な

sanctions：制裁

Critics：批判する人たち

homeland：国土

theocratic state：神政国家

Supreme Court：最高裁判所

communal violence：対立住民間の暴力

on his watch：彼の当番の時に

top official：知事

Citizenship Amendment Act：改正国籍法

Sikh：シーク教徒《パンジャーブ地方の宗教；合理的、現実的、寛容な教えが特徴》

Parsee：パーシー教徒《インドに住むゾロアスター教徒（拝火教教徒）》

Jain：ジャイナ教徒《「不害」の禁戒を厳守するなど徹底した苦行・禁欲主義が特徴》

left off：除外された
persecuted：迫害されている

Exercises

次の１〜５の英文を完成させるために、ａ〜ｄの中から最も適切なものを１つ選びなさい。

1. Kashmir's Muslims are incensed because

    a. Prime Minister Modi rounded up thousands of Muslims and revoked Kashmir's autonomy.

    b. two million illegal migrants in northeastern India were given citizenship.

    c. of recent comments about India by United Nations.

    d. of all of the above events.

2. India's Muslims are complaining of

    a. the government pursuing a Hindu national program.

    b. the increasingly secular character of the Modi government.

    c. discrimination by international organizations and religious groups.

    d. all of the above developments.

3. Currently India's population is

    a. 14% Muslim and 80% Hindu.

    b. 14% Hindu and 80% Muslim.

    c. 40% Hindu and 60% Muslim.

    d. 60% Hindu and 40% Muslim.

4. The new citizenship legislation that Prime Minister Modi wanted will expedite citizenship for migrants

    a. practicing Hinduism or Christianity.

    b. belonging to the Shia sect.

    c. from Kashmir's Muslim community.

    d. fleeing persecution by Christians.

5. Supporters of Prime Minster Modi's policies include

    a. United Nations officials.

    b. American representatives.

    c. radical Hindus nationalists.

    d. all of the above political and religious interests.

本文の内容に合致するものにＴ（True）、合致しないものにＦ（False）をつけなさい。

(   ) **1.** Prime Minister Modi has previously never used violence during his rule.

(   ) **2.** Protests within the Muslim community have broken out to complain about the anti-Muslim policies.

(   ) **3.** Progressives in India want a secular government for India and its future.

(   ) **4.** The new citizenship bill may not pass in Parliament.

(   ) **5.** When Mr. Modi was the top official in Gujarat in 2002, fighting between Muslims and Hindus cost 1,000 people their lives.

Vocabulary

次の１〜８は、イスラム教とヒンドゥ教、仏教に関する語です。下のａ〜ｈの説明文の中から最も適切なものを１つ選び、（   ）内に記入しなさい。

1. burka   (   )
2. Hinduism   (   )
3. Islam   (   )
4. Koran   (   )
5. nirvana   (   )
6. Ramadan   (   )
7. reincarnation   (   )
8. Siva   (   )

a. a state of knowledge reached while meditating
b. the ninth month of the Muslim year, during which no food or drink may be taken between sunrise and sunset
c. the predominant religion of the Indian subcontinent
d. the holy book of the Muslims
e. a long enveloping garment worn in public by Muslim women
f. the destroyer; one of the three Hindu major divinities
g. returning to life in a new body after death
h. the Muslim religion, and the people and countries that practice this religion

●急激な変化：ガイアナは石油で裕福になったが、民族間の緊張も増大

農業国から産油国へと急激に変化しつつあるガイアナの首都ジョージタウンの護岸沿いに建設中のビル群　　　Photo: The New York Times ／ Redux ／アフロ

Before you read

Republic of Guyana
ガイアナ共和国
1966年英国より独立

面積　215,000km²（本州よりやや小さい）（世界83位）
人口　783,000人（世界164位）
公用語　英語、ガイアナ・クレオール語
首都　ジョージタウン
民族　東インド系　39.8%
　　　アフリカ系　29.3%
　　　混血　19.9%
　　　先住民族　10.5%　／その他　0.5%
宗教　キリスト教カトリック　8.1%
　　　　　　　プロテスタント　16.9%
　　　　　　　イギリス国教会　6.9%
　　　ヒンドゥ教　28.4%
　　　イスラム教　7.2%
GDI　38億9900万米ドル（世界159位）
　　　1人当たり GDI　4,984米ドル（世界104位）
通貨　ガイアナ・ドル
政体　立憲共和制
識字率　85.6%

次の１〜５の語の説明として最も近いものをa〜eから１つ選び、（　　）内に記入しなさい。

1. sprawling　　　（　　）　　　a. low-lying and extensive
2. shrub　　　　　（　　）　　　b. poorly-built house
3. shack　　　　　（　　）　　　c. causing great harm to
4. devastating　　（　　）　　　d. bush or small tree
5. paralysis　　　（　　）　　　e. inability to act

Summary

次の英文は記事の要約です。下の語群から最も適切な語を１つ選び、（　　）内に記入しなさい。

80

　　Guyana hopes to transform its poor, (　　　　　　) economy by exploiting its oil resources. While many citizens see prospects for new (　　　　　), those making a living from sugar cane production are unhappy, with thousands of them now (　　　　　). Despite government promises to (　　　　　) sugar workers, the opposition says rural (　　　　　) are dying.

agricultural　　　communities　　　retrain　　　unemployed　　　wealth

　　ガイアナ共和国は、1966年５月に英連邦の１国として独立した。南アメリカ大陸で唯一英語が公用語の国である。1498年コロンブスが渡来、翌99年にヴェスプッチが上陸した。イギリス人の入植が行われたが、1621年以降は、オランダ西インド会社の管轄下に入り、18世紀までオランダの植民地となった。1814年からイギリスの植民地となり、British Guiana となった。奴隷制度廃止後、インド系移民が34万人近く流入し、サトウキビ農園労働者となった。

　　独立後、黒人勢力を代表する人民国民会議 PNC とインド系で社会主義の人民進歩党 PPP との間で人種的対立が起こり、政情不安が続いている。総選挙の度に暴動が起き、2020年３月の選挙でも両党の中傷が止まず、支持層への偏った利益誘導や人種対立で分断に拍車がかかった。

　　米石油エクソンモービルが、2015年に首都ジョージタウンの200km 沖合に海底油田を発見し、19年12月に原油生産を開始した。推定埋蔵量は80億バレルに上ると言われている。IMF は、2020年の経済成長率が前年の4.4％から85.6％に急上昇すると予測している。しかし、新型コロナウイルスの流行で移動制限や経済活動の停滞、原油価格の低下が影を落としている。さらに人種対立も収まっていない。

Reading

81

'It Changed So Fast': Oil Is Making Guyana Wealthy but Intensifying Tensions

Intensifying 〜：〜を強める

GEORGETOWN, Guyana — On a sprawling abandoned sugar estate by the coast of Guyana, the scale of the changes sweeping across the country is immediately visible.

sugar estate：砂糖農園

In just a few years, enormous warehouses and office
5 buildings servicing international oil companies have sprung up amid the shrub land, irrigation canals and fields of wild cane.

wild cane：野生のサトウキビ

82

People are "moving from cutting cane to businessmen," said Mona Harisha, a local shop owner. "It changed so fast."

10 Guyana is giving up its past as an agricultural economy and speeding toward its near-term future as an oil-producing giant. And so Ms. Harisha has renovated her general goods shop, redolent of Indian spices, which she runs from a side of her cottage in the Houston neighborhood of Georgetown, the
15 county's capital.

agricultural economy：農業経済国

giant：強国

from a side of 〜：〜の一角で

Houston neighborhood：ヒューストン地区

For many, the transformation into an oil economy has brought optimism about greater prosperity. But that optimism is often mixed with a fatalism that nothing will really improve for the vast majority of people in one of South America's
20 poorest countries.

optimism：楽観主義

fatalism：運命論

83

In a brick shack on the edge of the jungle 15 miles away from Houston, Jason Bobb-Semple, 25, is making his own big bet on oil.

making a big bet on 〜：〜に大きな賭けをする

With a $3,000 government loan, he built a small poultry
25 farm and bought 4,000 chicks to meet what he expects to be a booming food demand in a rapidly developing country.

poultry farm：養鶏場

meet 〜：〜を満たす、〜に対応する

food demand：食糧需要

Just hours after Mr. Bobb-Semple received the chicks, he got a visit from his first potential investor, a Guyanese émigré businessman who was back home looking for eggs to sell to
30 the offshore oil rigs.

potential investor：投資者になりそうな人

Guyanese émigré：ガイアナから外国に移住（亡命）した人

The investor, Lancelot Myers, said oil companies currently have to import most of their provisions, providing a business opportunity to local entrepreneurs who can fill supply gaps. "Now is the time to hit the ground running," he said.

35 The enterprising energy of the Guyanese seeking to benefit from the oil boom contrasts sharply with the deep depression, both economic and psychological, reining in the rural sugar belt, which had powered this country's economy since the 17th century.

40 A decision by the current president, David A. Granger, to shut down most of Guyana's unprofitable, state-owned cane processing plants in 2018 left about 7,000 sugar workers unemployed, devastating the surrounding regions.

The closures have turned places like Skeldon in the fertile
45 east of the country into ghost towns, wiping out the once vibrant local markets and businesses that used to serve the sugar workers.

The layoffs inflamed ethnic tensions, with the mainly Indo-Guyanese sugar workers accusing the predominantly black
50 government of Mr. Granger of targeted economic repression.

The ruling party advocates using the money to retrain agricultural workers for the public and service sectors. The opposition instead wants to subsidize sugar farms to keep rural communities alive.

55 The International Monetary Fund projected that Guyana's tiny economy would grow by 86 percent this year, the fastest rate in the world. That forecast, however, is likely to take a major hit from the sudden collapse of oil prices, the coronavirus pandemic and Guyana's ongoing political paralysis.

The New York Times, April 7, 2020

provisions：食糧

supply gaps：供給ギャップ

hit the ground running：新しいことに直ぐに全力で取り組む

reining in 〜：〜を抑える、弱める

cane processing plants：サトウキビ加工工場

used to 〜：かつては〜していた

layoffs：一時解雇

ethnic tensions：民族間の緊張

Indo-Guyanese：インド系ガイアナ人《1834年に奴隷制度が廃止されると、砂糖工場の労働者としてインド人が導入された》

accusing 〜 of …：〜を…だと非難する

targeted economic repression：自分たちを標的にした経済的抑圧

ruling party：与党

the money：石油収入

public sector：公共部門

subsidize 〜：〜に助成金を払う

International Monetary Fund：国際通貨基金 (IMF)《国際金融や為替相場の安定化を目的として設立された国際連合の専門機関》

fastest rate：最大の伸び率

take a major hit from 〜：〜によって大損害を被る

collapse：暴落

ongoing：現在進行中の

paralysis：マヒ状態

Exercises

Multiple Choice

次の１～２の英文の質問に答え、３～５の英文を完成させるために、ａ～ｄの中から最も適切なものを１つ選びなさい。

1. What has changed in Guyana?

    a. Poultry farms are all over the city.

    b. Sugar canes estates are now flourishing.

    c. There is a new oil economy.

    d. The economy has grown by 86%.

2. What occurred when David Granger shut down sugar cane estates?

    a. Citizens started purchasing more chickens.

    b. 7,000 workers lost their jobs.

    c. The government supplied new jobs for displaced workers.

    d. The employment patterns of agricultural workers went unchanged.

3. Guyana is changing into an oil economy, which means

    a. there is a chance of greater prosperity.

    b. many citizens are expecting a more comfortable life.

    c. some citizens are likely to get left behind.

    d. all of the above developments are expected.

4. Mr. Bobb-Semple's chicken investment

    a. has failed because people can no longer afford to buy eggs.

    b. seems to be paying off now that he is to supply eggs to the oil rigs.

    c. has badly affected the economy of towns like Skeldon.

    d. seems likely to end in financial disaster.

5. Guyana has been involved in the process of sugar cane since

    a. the 16th century.

    b. the 17th century.

    c. the 18th century.

    d. the 19th century.

本文の内容に合致するものに T（True）、合致しないものに F（False）をつけなさい。

(   ) **1.** Guyana's ruling party says it will retrain agricultural workers for public sector and service employment.

(   ) **2.** The opposition wants to subsidize sugar to keep rural towns alive.

(   ) **3.** Local markets and business in most rural towns continue to thrive.

(   ) **4.** The International Monetary Fund predictions for Guyana's growth look to be fairly accurate.

(   ) **5.** There is currently a recession in parts of Guyana caused by the changes in their economy.

Vocabulary

次の１〜８の英文は、貧富に関することわざです。日本文に合わせて、下の語群の中から最も適切な語を１つ選び、（　　）内に記入しなさい。

1. 金がものを言う世の中だ。
Money is (   ) in this world of ours.

2. 貧乏くじを引いてしまった。
He drew the short (   ).

3. 金に糸目をつけない。
He is (   ) with his money.

4. 金持ち苦労多し。
Much coin, much (   ).

5. 金の切れ目が縁の切れ目。
When poverty comes in, love (   ) out of the windows.

6. 金持ちの食道楽、貧乏人の子沢山。
Rich men feed, poor men (   ).

7. 金持ち喧嘩せず。
A rich man never (   ).

8. 貧乏暇なし。
Poor men have no (   ).

breed	care	everything	flies
free	leisure	quarrels	straw

Unit 15

● カルロス・ゴーンの大脱走劇

2019年3月、保釈されて東京拘置所を出る日産
自動車の前会長カルロス・ゴーン被告

Photo: Kyodo News

Before you read

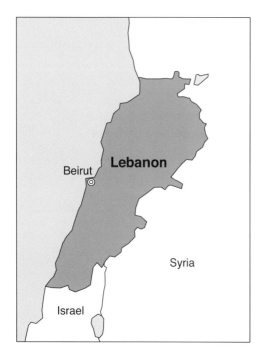

Lebanese Republic
レバノン共和国

面積　10,452km²（岐阜県とほぼ同じ）（世界161位）
首都・最大都市　ベイルート
公用語　アラビア語（フランス語と英語も通用）
人口　6,856,000人（世界108位）
民族　アラブ人　95%
　　　アルメニア人　4%
宗教　キリスト教（マロン派 ／ ギリシャ正教 ／ ギ
　　　リシャ・カトリック ／カトリック ／
　　　アルメニア正教）40.4%
　　　イスラム教　54%
　　　ドゥルーズ派　5.6%
識字率　87.4%
GDP　563.72億ドル（世界82位）
　　　1人当たりのGDP　9,251ドル（世界76位）
通貨　レバノン・ポンド
政体　共和制

次の１〜５の語句の説明として最も近いものをa〜eから１つ選び、（　）内に記入しなさい。

1. fugitive　　　　（　　）
2. procedural　　　（　　）
3. hands-on　　　　（　　）
4. infringe　　　　（　　）
5. conceal　　　　　（　　）

a. active
b. a person escaping from the law
c. disobey or violate
d. hide
e. administrative or bureaucratic

Summary

　次の英文は記事の要約です。下の語群から最も適切な語を１つ選び、（　　）内に記入しなさい。

86

　Facing (　　　　　) from Nissan, and (　　　　　) who win almost every case, Carlos Ghosn made escape plans that seemed (　　　　) to succeed. In the relaxed days before New Year, with private security forces temporarily (　　　　　), he took a train to Kansai Airport and flew off in a private jet, (　　　　) in a case too large for the x-ray machines.

hidden　　hostility　　prosecutors　　unlikely　　withdrawn

　　1954年ブラジル生まれの Carlos Ghosn カルロス・ゴーンは45歳の時、日産自動車の最高執行責任者に就任した。その後、日産自動車の社長兼最高経営責任者、ルノーの取締役会長兼最高経営責任者、ルノー・日産アライアンスの会長兼最高経営責任者に就任した。
　　カルロスの祖父は、13歳のときレバノンからブラジルに移住した。父親はブラジル生まれでナイジェリア出身のレバノン人女性と結婚した。カルロスが６歳のとき、母親と３人の姉妹と共にレバノンのベイルートに転居し、小・中学校教育はベイルートで受け、高校はパリで学び、1974年、20歳でエリート養成校 Ecole Polytechnique を卒業し、24歳で Ecole des Mines de Paris で工学博士を取得した。24歳でタイヤメーカーのミシュランに入社し、30歳で南米ミシュラン最高執行責任者、36歳で北米の最高経営責任者に昇格した。1996年にルノーの上席副社長にヘッドハンティングされ、1999年にルノーと日産の資本提携後、ルノーの役職も兼任しながら日産の最高執行責任者に就任した。
　　2018年11月、東京地検特捜部により金融商品取引法違反容疑で逮捕された。19年４月に特別背任の容疑で４度目の逮捕となったが、再度保釈された。同年12月29日に海外渡航を禁じた裁判所の保釈条件を破り、日本を秘密裏に出国、プライベートジェットでトルコを経由し、31日の朝ベイルート国際空港に到着した。

Reading

The Great Escape: How Carlos Ghosn became the world's most famous fugitive

fugitive：逃亡犯人

SINGAPORE / LONDON / TOKYO / PARIS — Ghosn's prospects of proving his innocence in Japan were dismal. Prosecutors there win more than 99 percent of the cases they try and enjoy a wide range of procedural advantages. Against
5 Ghosn, who was facing potential sentences of more than a decade in prison, they had an even greater-than-usual asset: the full co-operation of Nissan, which had repeatedly made clear its determination to see him convicted and had provided a huge trove of documents as well as hands-on investigative
10 assistance.

prospects：見通し
innocence：無実
dismal：暗い
Prosecutors：検察官
cases they try：彼らが裁判にかける訴訟（事例）
enjoy ～：～に恵まれている
sentences：判決
asset：有用なもの
convicted：有罪宣告を受ける
hands-on：現場での

Ghosn, however, had another option — a desperate play, months in the planning, that might restore some portion of his freedom if everything went right, or send him straight back to a 7-meter-square (75-foot-square) cell in Tokyo if any aspect
15 went awry.

desperate play：一か八かの捨て身の行動

cell：独房
any aspect went awry：ある局面で失敗したら

On its face, it must have seemed like a ridiculous idea.

On its face：一見

Yet there was a clear window of opportunity: New Year's, when government offices can close for more than a week and even the most hard-boiled prosecutors and police
20 detectives take time off to be with their families. His lawyers had recently threatened to file a complaint against a private security company hired by Nissan to follow him, claiming it was infringing illegally on his rights. According to a person familiar with the situation, the company's agents had backed
25 off as a result — at least temporarily.

police detectives：刑事

file a complaint against ～：～を告訴する
follow ～：～を監視する
infringing on ～：～を侵害している
agents：スパイ

If Ghosn was going to escape, this was the moment to do it. But he needed the right help.

In the shadowy world of private-security contractors, Michael Taylor was a swashbuckler who stood out. He
30 protected powerful people and companies, secretly helped the U.S. government investigate crimes, and admitted breaking

swashbuckler：無法者、悪漢

88 Unit 15

the law himself.

For the Ghosn operation, Taylor had a partner, a Lebanese-born man named George-Antoine Zayek.

35　On the morning of Sunday, Dec. 29, Taylor and Zayek arrived in a Bombardier Global Express Jet — a plane with a range of more than 11,000 kilometers (6,800 miles) — at the private-jet terminal of Kansai International Airport, a busy hub built on an artificial island near Osaka. There were also
40　two large black cases on board, according to people familiar with the flight who asked not to be identified.

Later the same day, according to security camera footage reported on by Japanese media, Ghosn walked out the front door of his house, wearing a hat and a surgical-style face
45　mask. He then took a bullet train from Tokyo's Shinagawa Station to Osaka at about 4:30 p.m. local time and, after the journey, took a cab to a hotel near the airport, the network NTV reported.

Outbound passengers at the private terminal aren't exempt
50　from passport control, and according to people familiar with airport operations, there were customs and immigration officials present before the Bombardier's departure. But Ghosn wasn't boarding as an official passenger. He was, apparently, cargo, concealed in a large black case that, according to the
55　people, was too big to fit into the airport's X-ray machines. With nothing obviously amiss, the jet was in the air by 11:10 p.m.

The Japan Times based on Bloomberg, January 8, 2020

operation：作戦

Bombardier Global Express
　Jet：《カナダのボンバル
　ディア・エアロスペース
　社開発の大型ビジネスジ
　ェット機》
range：航続距離
busy hub：離発着便の多い
　ハブ空港

asked not to be identified：
　匿名希望の

bullet train：新幹線

NTV：日本テレビ《Nippon
　Television》
Outbound：出国する
exempt from 〜：〜を免除
　される
passport control：出入国審査
customs and immigration
　officials：税関・出入国
　管理局職員
present：立ち会う
cargo：貨物
the people：関係者

amiss：間違った

Exercises

次の１〜３の英文の質問に答え、４〜５の英文を完成させるために、ａ〜ｄの中から最も適切なものを１つ選びなさい。

1. If convicted, how much prison time might Ghosn have to serve?

    a. Ten years.
    b. Fifteen years.
    c. Twenty years.
    d. Twenty-five years.

2. How did Ghosn get on the plane?

    a. He was placed in a large cargo box that was too large to fit through the x-ray machine.
    b. He walked onto the plane disguised as a woman.
    c. He took a taxi to the airport and met his 'handlers.'
    d. The article does not go into any detail about this mystery.

3. Who assisted Ghosn in arranging plans for his escape from the country?

    a. His family members.
    b. Michael Taylor and George-Antoine Zayek.
    c. Several associates from Nissan who were "in his corner."
    d. A private security company that was hired to follow him.

4. Nissan seems to have been

    a. very keen to cooperate fully with the prosecution.
    b. willing to provide documents in their possession to get Ghosn convicted.
    c. hoping Ghosn would stand trial in Japan.
    d. taking all of the above stances in the period before Ghosn escaped.

5. Ghosn's chances of being acquitted are said to be

    a. excellent.
    b. fifty-fifty.
    c. gloomy.
    d. somewhat slim.

本文の内容に合致するものにT（True）、合致しないものにF（False）をつけなさい。

(   ) **1.** The conviction rate of legal cases in Japan is at least 99%.

(   ) **2.** The plane took off from the private jet terminal at Kansai Airport.

(   ) **3.** Michael Taylor is described in the article as a swashbuckler, a word usually used for pirates.

(   ) **4.** The plan to escape Japan was made very quickly.

(   ) **5.** Ghosn managed to avoid passport control by walking onto the plane in disguise.

Vocabulary

次の英文は、the Japan Times に掲載された *Once a hero in Japan, Carlos Ghosn's news conference unlikely to restore his image*『日本で英雄だったカルロス・ゴーンの記者会見も彼のイメージ回復にはならないようだ』の記事の一部です。下の語群から最も適切なものを１つ選び、（   ）内に記入しなさい。

In an extraordinary news conference 14 months in the making, Carlos Ghosn (   ) Nissan Motor Co. executives, Japanese prosecutors and the nation's (   ) system in what was a watershed moment for a corporate crime drama that has made global headlines and stirred talks of a Hollywood production.

By (   ) to Lebanon and thus (   ) himself from the legal risks that would have come from speaking to the media in Japan, the former Nissan chairman was granted his long-held wish to provide his own account in his own words. He made full use of the opportunity – speaking for an hour before (   ) questions from reporters – and covered topics including harrowing accounts of his detention, while also (   ) Nissan executives that he says had a role in bringing him down.

While international media has focused much of its coverage on criticisms of the Japanese criminal justice system, domestic media outlets have been more critical of Ghosn (   ) bail conditions and leaving the country without facing trial.

answering	fleeing	freeing	justice
lambasted	outing	violating	

15章版：ニュースメディアの英語

──演習と解説2021年度版──

検印 省略	©2021年 1 月31日　　初 版 発 行

編著者　　　　　　　高 橋 　 優 身

　　　　　　　　　　伊 藤 　 典 子

　　　　　　　　Richard　Powell

発行者　　　　　　　原 　 雅 　 久

発行所　　　　　　株式会社朝日出版社

101-0065　東京都千代田区西神田3-3-5

電話 (03) 3239-0271

FAX (03) 3239-0479

e-mail: text-e@asahipress.com

振替口座　00140-2-46008

組版・製版／信毎書籍印刷株式会社

ISBN 978-4-255-15664-4 C1082

ちょっと手ごわい、でも効果絶大！
最強のリスニング強化マガジン

 **ENGLISH EXPRESS**

音声ダウンロード付き　毎月6日発売　定価（本体1,148円＋税）

定期購読をお申し込みの方には
本誌1号分無料ほか、特典多数。
詳しくは下記ホームページへ。

英語が楽しく続けられる！

重大事件から日常のおもしろネタ、
スターや著名人のインタビューなど、
CNNの多彩なニュースを
生の音声とともにお届けします。
3段階ステップアップ方式で
初めて学習する方も安心。
どなたでも楽しく続けられて
実践的な英語力が身につきます。

資格試験の強い味方！

ニュース英語に慣れれば、TOEIC®テストや英検の
リスニング問題も楽に聞き取れるようになります。

CNN ENGLISH EXPRESS ホームページ

英語学習に役立つコンテンツが満載！

［本誌のホームページ］https://ee.asahipress.com/
［編集部のTwitter］https://twitter.com/asahipress_ee

朝日出版社 〒101-0065 東京都千代田区西神田 3-3-5　TEL 03-3263-3321